Promises And Perils Of Artificial General Intelligence

Practical Advances in
Artificial Intelligence and Machine Learning

Dr. Lance B. Eliot, MBA, PhD

Disclaimer: This book is presented solely for educational and entertainment purposes. The author and publisher are not offering it as legal, accounting, or other professional services advice. The author and publisher make no representations or warranties of any kind and assume no liabilities of any kind with respect to the accuracy or completeness of the contents and specifically disclaim any implied warranties of merchantability or fitness of use for a particular purpose. Neither the author nor the publisher shall be held liable or responsible to any person or entity with respect to any loss or incidental or consequential damages caused, or alleged to have been caused, directly or indirectly, by the information or programs contained herein. Every company is different, and the advice and strategies contained herein may not be suitable for your situation.

ISBN: 978-1-95-738621-8

DEDICATION

To my incredible daughter, Lauren, and my incredible son, Michael.

Forest fortuna adiuvat (from the Latin; good fortune favors the brave).

CONTENTS

ACKNOWLEDGMENTS

I have been the beneficiary of advice and counsel from many friends, colleagues, family, investors, and many others. I want to thank everyone who has aided me throughout my career. I write from the heart and the head, having experienced first-hand what it means to have others around you who support you during the good times and the tough times.

To Warren Bennis, one of my doctoral advisors and ultimately a colleague, I offer my deepest thanks and appreciation, especially for his calm and insightful wisdom and support.

To Mark Stevens and his generous efforts toward funding and supporting the USC Stevens Center for Innovation.

To Lloyd Greif and the USC Lloyd Greif Center for Entrepreneurial Studies for their ongoing encouragement of founders and entrepreneurs.

To Peter Drucker, William Wang, Aaron Levie, Peter Kim, Jon Kraft, Cindy Crawford, Jenny Ming, Steve Milligan, Chis Underwood, Frank Gehry, Buzz Aldrin, Steve Forbes, Bill Thompson, Dave Dillon, Alan Fuerstman, Larry Ellison, Jim Sinegal, John Sperling, Mark Stevenson, Anand Nallathambi, Thomas Barrack, Jr., and many other innovators and leaders that I have met and gained mightily from doing so.

Thanks to Ed Trainor, Kevin Anderson, James Hickey, Wendell Jones, Ken Harris, DuWayne Peterson, Mike Brown, Jim Thornton, Abhi Beniwal, Al Biland, John Nomura, Eliot Weinman, John Desmond, and many others for their unwavering support during my career.

And most of all thanks as always to Lauren and Michael, for their ongoing support and for having seen me writing and heard much of this material during the many months involved in writing it. To their patience and willingness to listen.

CHAPTER 1
INTRODUCTION TO AI AND AGI

This book is about getting from AI (artificial intelligence) to AGI (artificial general intelligence). When I generally herein refer to AI, I am primarily talking about the kind of AI that we have currently, such as the widely popular generative AI and large language models (LLMs). That's fine stuff, but it isn't the aspirational kind of AI. The big-time aspirational AI is known as AGI and would be a lot more advanced than today's AI.

AGI is a future type of AI that we hope to devise and would be on par with human intellect in all respects. We don't have that yet. No worries, since hope springs eternal that we will somehow progress existing AI to become AGI.

Please know that there isn't any kind of clear-cut blueprint or laid-out map that precisely says how we will go from today's conventional AI to the someday envisioned AGI. Nobody really knows how we will attain AGI. Indeed, we might not achieve AGI or maybe AGI is so far off in the future that we won't be around when it is attained.

But that doesn't stop us from trying our best right now to anticipate AGI and do whatever we can to arrive at AGI.

I have been writing extensively about AI and AGI for many years in my globally popular column on AI trends for *Forbes*. In addition, I perform consulting for AI makers and other firms that are striving to arrive at AGI. I teach classes about AI and AGI, having formerly been a professor, and continue my scholarly pursuits on these weighty matters too.

My writing style combines both the scholarly perspective on these topics and is conjoined with the practical aspects too. The aim is to be engaging, factual, highly readable, and notably informative. The material here will readily get you up-to-speed and I hope will inspire you to join this exciting and rapidly evolving field of endeavor.

The chapters are a curated collection of my best expositions on AI and AGI. You are welcome to read the chapters in any order you prefer. This first chapter gets you ready for the rest of the material. Each of the subsequent chapters generally stands on its own. Once you've got this introductory foundation under your belt, you are good to proceed. An addendum has suggestions for using this book in classroom settings.

As an overall perspective on AGI, think about time and three crucial eras:

- **(i) Pre-AGI**: The time we are in now.
- **(ii) Attained-AGI**: A time we aim for but don't know when it will occur.
- **(iii) Post-AGI**: The time after AGI has been attained and the ramifications that will accordingly ensue.

The chapters variously address those three eras. Without further ado, let's get underway with some vital foundational aspects.

Foundational Aspects Of AI And AGI

It might seem surprising to discover that the definition of AI is not nailed down, nor is the definition of AGI solidified. At first glance, a definitional disparity might seem of little consequence. A rose is a rose, one might insist, no matter how it is defined. The problem though is that if you don't know what a rose is then there is ample room to talk past each other when discussing roses. For some, a rose might really be an apple, while others might believe it to be an orange.

The practical concerns are aplenty when it comes to the vagueness and variability of what AI and AGI denote.

For example, there is a great deal of concern these days about AI or AGI being an existential risk, namely that we might be all wiped out or enslaved by intelligent machines. This has brought forth calls to stridently rein in AI and AGI. Indeed, there are AI ethics guidelines or soft laws that attempt to ensure that AI or AGI is devised in a responsible manner and aligned with human values, generally referred to as Responsible AI.

But tons of loopholes make this a very leaky ship.

The vexing issue is that the definition or meaning of AI or AGI in those governing efforts could be exasperatingly off-target. If a devised definition is overly broad, we could have all kinds of non-AI apps and systems that suddenly are being burdened by new laws or stipulated guidelines that were supposed to cover just AI or AGI. Innovation could be inadvertently stifled. If the definitions undershoot what AI or AGI is, the result could be that threatening types of AI and AGI might escape the stipulated governance constraints by being considered outside the scope of the freshly devised AI laws. They will run free, as it were, unencumbered by laws that lamentedly imbue slipshod or loosey-goosey definitions.

Furthermore, I've predicted that we are going to get into a long-term and excruciatingly costly legal battle once these new AI laws begin to be enforced.

Here's the deal.

A company that allegedly has devised an AI or AGI app will be dragged into the courts under the claim that the app violates some particular new AI law. The lawyers for that company will strenuously argue that the definition of AI or AGI in that passed law does not squarely match the nature of the app that the firm has devised. Back and forth the protracted legal arguments will go. You can bet that these issues will eventually climb up the legal ladder in the appeals process (taking years to slog forward).

It is conceivable that at some point the U.S. Supreme Court might need to weigh in, especially if these laws convey some form of legal agency to AI or AGI of their own standing.

Defining AI And AGI As Best We Can

You certainly have heard or seen the AI moniker. It's everywhere these days. You might sometimes have seen or heard the AGI moniker. It has been gradually gaining momentum.

The phrase "Artificial Intelligence" and its abbreviation of AI have been around since the start of this field of study in the 1950s. In contrast, the phrase "Artificial General Intelligence" abbreviated as AGI has only been around for roughly twenty years or so (there are debates about the precise moment that the AGI naming originated, though most would likely concede that the AGI moniker wasn't a widely public-known popularized phrase until the last five to ten years).

If you are unsure of the difference between referring to something as AI versus saying that it is AGI, you can rest assured that you are not alone in that bewilderedness. As I said, these definitions are all over the map. That being said, I am going to try and somewhat straighten that out for you. Hang in there and you'll get some semblance of clarity on this.

First, let's begin at the beginning by noting what is meant by the AI moniker and how it came to arise as an everyday parlance. Second, I will shift into examining the somewhat more recently devised AGI moniker and explain how that naming came to be. Third, I'll explore how a prominent AI maker, called DeepMind proposes how AGI might be better understood as a construct by utilizing levels of autonomy.

On The Meaning Of AI

I am frequently asked during my many speaking engagements at AI conferences a rather pointed question as to what AI is or what is the definition of AI. This query is certainly understandable. Such a question vividly showcases the prevailing confusion over the matter. It seems that each resource that you might refer to online has a different definition of AI. A colossally frustrating circumstance for all.

I usually try to be as succinct as I reasonably can and simply indicate that AI refers to systems that exhibit intelligent behavior. Period, end of story. Well, of course, that's not really the end of the story and there is a lot more involved. I find that giving a rough-and-tumble definition is typically all that most people seem to informally want to know. In that sense, if you like, you can just declare that AI is about systems that exhibit intelligent behavior and then drop the mic. I doubt though that this will be entirely satisfying for those with an innate sense of curiosity.

We shall go ahead and use this brisk definition to get things started:

- "AI is a system that exhibits intelligent behavior."

Let's parse this basic conception.

Right away you can ask a provocative and logically important question as to what is meant by the notion of intelligent behavior. Does a toaster exhibit intelligent behavior? A modern-day toaster seems to be able to toast bread and stop doing so when the bread is toasted. Isn't that intelligence at work? I doubt that we would generally say that a conventional toaster is intelligent enough to be within the realm of any overall sense of what might be construed as AI.

The question then arises as to what we mean by intelligence, intelligent behavior, and the like.

Another important parsing is that the short and sweet definition says that AI exhibits intelligent behavior, which is a stark contrast to saying that AI *embodies* intelligent behavior. Here's why that is a crucial distinction. We usually indicate that humans embody intelligence. Somehow, and we don't truly yet know how, humans in their brains are able to embody intelligence. AI as we conceive of it today is a mathematical and computational formulation consisting of hardware and software. It is not the same as the wetware of our brains and our minds.

Thus, rather than saying that AI embodies intelligence per se, which might be anthropomorphizing the AI, we would be better off saying that AI *exhibits* intelligent behavior. The AI might be of an entirely different construct than what happens in the human brain. And that's okay.

We don't necessarily have to do precisely what the underlying mechanism of the brain does. If we can arrive at the same or similar outcomes, namely the exhibiting of intelligent behavior, we have won the brass ring.

Some AI researchers want to exactly create in computers the same constructs of what the brain does, either feature- for-feature or do a simulation of it. They aim to reverse engineer the brain and the mind. Doing so will hopefully make things more apparent as to devising AI that does the same kind of things.

Other AI researchers believe that we don't necessarily have to crack the secret code on how the brain and the human mind work. They point out that if you are relying on exposing the inner secrets of the biological and chemical mysteries of the brain, you might be bottlenecked trying to arrive at AI. The idea is that maybe we can come up with intelligent behaviors by doing something akin to the brain or perhaps even something utterly unlike the brain. If we could piece together Legos and get intelligent behavior, this would be miraculous and presumably not dependent on divining how the human mind functions.

Okay, so the shortest kind of definition for AI is that systems exhibiting intelligent behavior are construed as being what we will label as AI. For the moment, we'll leave vague the understanding of what intelligent behavior consists of. The overall emphasis is that the AI just has to exhibit and not necessarily embody whatever mechanisms give rise to showcasing intelligent behavior.

Shift gears and let's proceed toward lengthier definitions of AI.

Mentally go back in time to the 1950s.

A hallmark for when the AI phrase first began is considered found within a proposal for a research project in 1955 that sought to explore something new that was coined as artificial intelligence. The proposal was put together by computer scientist John McCarthy and had this subject title (note that the title mentions "artificial intelligence"): "A Proposal for the Dartmouth Summer Research Project On Artificial Intelligence", by John McCarthy, M. L. Minsky, N. Rochester, and C.E. Shannon, dated August 31, 1955.

John McCarty is often designated as the considered father of AI.

Here is a notable excerpt from the cited proposal:

- "The study is to proceed on the basis of the conjecture that every aspect of learning or any other feature of intelligence can in principle be so precisely described that a machine can be made to simulate it. An attempt will be made to find how to make machines use language, form abstractions and concepts, solve kinds of problems now reserved for humans, and improve themselves."

The excerpt implies that AI is that which consists of a machine that can be made to simulate intelligence.

The simulation doesn't have to be precisely what the brain or mind does. We can proceed on the basis that alternative means are satisfactory. The overarching goal is to devise machines that can do things that humans rely upon their respective intelligence to do, such as making use of natural languages, devising and utilizing abstractions and concepts, solving problems, and learning or improving upon the intelligence that we embody.

We can also consider what today's dictionaries say when it comes to defining AI.

Here is a smattering of AI definitions that I plucked from the Internet for today's column:

- "The capability of computer systems or algorithms to imitate intelligent human behavior" (source: Merriam-Webster Dictionary).

- "Artificial intelligence is a type of computer technology concerned with making machines work in an intelligent way, similar to the way that the human mind works" (source: Collins Dictionary).

- "The theory and development of computer systems able to perform tasks that normally require human intelligence, such as visual perception, speech recognition, decision-making, and translation between languages" (source: Oxford Languages Dictionary).

- The use or study of computer systems or machines that have some of the qualities that the human brain has, such as the ability to interpret and produce language in a way that seems human, recognize or create images, solve problems, and learn from data supplied to them" (source: Cambridge Dictionary).

I trust that you can discern some important characteristics of those short definitions of AI. By and large, they steer clear of insisting that AI must be exactly composed as the human brain or mind is composed. The indication is that exhibiting intelligence or simulating intelligence is sufficient.

Another common element of AI definitions involves trying to explain what is meant by intelligent behaviors. For example, one or more of those dictionary definitions attempts to explain that intelligent behavior might be the ability to recognize or create images. The 1955 proposal also laid out some explanatory examples such as being able to solve problems and learn languages. Giving examples of what is meant by intelligent behavior is handy and somewhat gets us around the toaster conundrum. Currently, toasters aren't able to generally solve problems (other than toasting!), though in the future you are likely to see that AI-infused toasters will gradually become more common -- I'll have to change up my toaster comparison accordingly.

Maybe I'll just ask my toaster to tell me what AI is.

Alleged Robust Definitions Of AI

You are now familiar with and hopefully feel conversant in the short-form definitions of AI. I've presented you with AI definitions that range from a few words in size to a sentence or two in size.

We are ready to move up to the bigwigs.

Attempts to define AI for legal purposes are often done by expanding the length of the definition.

The keystone assumption is that a few words or a sentence won't cut the mustard. We need to be more detailed about what AI is. The trouble with expanding the size of the wording is that you don't necessarily make things any tighter. There can be just as much variability in a lengthy definition as there can be in a shorter one.

Do not be fooled into thinking that the length of the definition alone imparts preciseness. It does not. All in all, words that we use in our natural language such as English are said to be semantically ambiguous. The upshot is that each word that we use can have a multitude of meanings. The more words that you toss into a definition, the more semantic ambiguity you will likely have.

Sometimes a kind of wording-oriented death spiral occurs. A definition is expanded with more and more words to try and pin down the semantic ambiguities and get a tighter definition. Meanwhile, for each additional word included, you are also increasing the semantic ambiguity. You can't win. There is some point at which a kind of crossover occurs. You have to settle on some final set of wording that aims to have enough words to reduce the ambiguities which at the same time doesn't open the door to even more ambiguities.

Makes one's head hurt to think about it.

In the United States, a frequently utilized legalese definition for AI is one that can be found in the U.S. National Defense Authorization Act and has been carried around for several years from its initial use to today. I'll show you it in a moment. Many other federal agencies use the same definition. Some states use it too. The thinking is that this is maybe a defacto AI definition that can be used on a copy-and-paste basis.

We do not yet know whether the definition will stand up to legal scrutiny. Just because it is often used doesn't make it airtight. The chances are that at some future time, the definition will get vetted in our courts. The result could be that all those others who have relied upon the definition will then be subject to whatever legally determined deficiency exists. They will all be in the same boat, rightly or wrongly. A ripping effect will occur. The dominos might fall all at once.

This doesn't imply or suggest that other AI definitions are any better off.

Those who try to reinvent the wheel of AI definitions are equally subject to legal exposure. Until or if we somehow arrive collectively at a universally agreed definition for AI, everyone is facing the same looming sword hanging over their heads.

Here then is the semi-default widely-copied AI definition as shown in the US National Defense Authorization Act:

- "A machine-based system that can for a given set of human-defined objectives, make predictions, recommendations or decisions influencing real or virtual environments. Artificial intelligence systems use machine and human-based inputs to: (a) Perceive real and virtual environments, (b) Abstract such perceptions into models through analysis in an automated manner, (c) Use model inference to formulate options for information or action" (source: United States National Defense Authorization Act, Fiscal Year 2024).

Take a close look at it.

You can readily see that it has the same hallmarks as the shorter AI definitions. The length is for sure longer. Does the length help or hurt? Well, there is a lot of debate about that. For example, the definition says that "for a given set of human-defined objectives" is part of the definition.

Ponder that segment.

If we have an AI system that is not provided with a set of human-defined objectives, does that mean that the AI system is not construed as an AI system since it averts the given definition? In other words, we let loose something that most of us would likely agree is in fact AI, but we do not feed it any stated objectives. Instead, we let it self-determine its objectives. Ergo, this would seem to no longer be an AI system as defined by this particular definition. It falls outside of the stated definition.

Do you see the quandary at hand?

I hope so.

You can pick apart the rest of the definitions in a similar fashion. This isn't being nit-picky. Keep in mind that the legal definition will have a wide significance in terms of what is construed as within the scope of AI. This in turn will determine what legally is susceptible to the constraints or limits associated with the law at hand. And so on.

You might be wondering whether we could arrive at a universal definition of AI that would cut across all borders and geographies. Does the United States really need to have its own definition of AI? The same could be said of Canada, France, the UK, and the like.

Does each country need to have its own definition?

Your gut instinct would be that there is no need to have a nation-specific AI definition. AI is AI, regardless of which country is contending with it. A rose is a rose, no matter which country the rose is found in. The problem though is that since AI is loosey-goosey at the get-go, each jurisdiction seems to want to define AI in their own preferred manner. This applies within the United States too, such that there are a multitude of federal definitions, and there are a multitude of AI definitions at the state level, and even the same can be said at the county level, the city level, and so on. There are enough definitions of AI to poke a stick at.

The EU has been working on a piece of legislation known as the EU Artificial Intelligence Act (AIA) and it too contains a definition of AI. This would be an AI definition that would presumably apply to a plethora of countries since it is aiming to be passed for the EU all told.

Here is the EU AIA definition of AI (subject to change since it is a draft):

- "A system that is designed to operate with elements of autonomy and that, based on machine and/or human-provided data and inputs, infers how to achieve a given set of human-defined objectives using machine learning and/or logic- and knowledge based approaches, and produces system-generated outputs such as content (generative AI systems), predictions, recommendations or decisions, influencing the environments with which the AI system interacts" (EU Artificial Intelligence Act, Draft 2022).

What do you think of that AI definition?

It certainly seems more technologically terminology-laden. The notion of generative AI is mentioned. The phrasing of knowledge-based systems is indicated. Etc. You might observe that the word "autonomy" is prominently noted too. We will return to the autonomy aspects later on in this discussion.

Despite the heavy use of terminology, be assured there are plenty of loopholes and gotchas in the drafted AI definition. It too is subject to semantic ambiguity, as are all definitions.

You might be wondering whether the United Nations has any AI definitions. The hope might be that a universal definition of AI could be landed upon at the UN level. Perhaps all other countries would then merely copy and paste that definition. Turns out that the UN has a multitude of AI definitions and confronts the same conundrum as the rest of us.

Here is an example of an AI definition as noted in the UNESCO document that depicts AI ethics considerations:

- "Information-processing technologies that integrate models and algorithms that produce a capacity to learn and to perform cognitive tasks leading to outcomes such as prediction and decision-making in material and virtual environments. AI systems are designed to operate with varying degrees of autonomy by means of knowledge modeling and representation and by exploiting data and calculating correlations. AI systems may include several methods, such as but not limited to: (i) machine learning, including deep learning and reinforcement learning; (ii) machine reasoning, including planning, scheduling, knowledge representation and reasoning, search, and optimization" (United Nations UNESCO, Recommendation on the Ethics of AI, 2021).

I realize you might be nearing a point of numbness about these various AI definitions.

I'll share one last one for now and encourage you to go online to find more. Plenty can be found.

This is what the OECD has offered as an AI definition (they have other AI definitions too):

- "A machine-based system that can, for a given set of human-defined objectives, make predictions, recommendations, or decisions influencing real or virtual environments. AI systems are designed to operate with varying levels of autonomy" (OECD Organization for Economic Co-operation and Development, Council on Artificial Intelligence).

Note again the use of the word autonomy.

We shall next consider additional caveats about AI definitions, including leading up to the autonomy elements.

Different Ways Of Referring To AI

One of the difficulties in nailing down what AI consists of involves the different ways in which AI as a moniker is typically used in society. This is reminiscent of the parable about the blind persons trying to describe an elephant. One person touches the tusk and insists that is what the elephant entails. Another person touches a stout leg and insists that is what the elephant entails. And on this goes.

Let's go ahead and get the mainstay of the elephant depictions of AI onto the open table.

Here are the four mainstays:

- **(1) AI is a computer system or machine (as an artifact).**
- **(2) AI is a field of study.**
- **(3) AI is a set of techniques and technologies.**
- **(4) AI is an aspiration or goal.**

Time to unpack those.

The first mainstay is akin to the definitions of AI that I've already covered, namely that AI is a computer system or machine. It is in a broad sense an artifact that can exhibit intelligent behavior.

The second mainstay considers AI to be a field of study. Similar to considering law or medicine as fields of study, one might liken AI to a domain or specialty that people can learn about, research on, teach, practice, and advance as an endeavor. A college student these days might get asked what they are majoring in and will sometimes say that they are majoring in AI.

The third mainstay asserts that AI can be described as numerous techniques or technologies. For example, AI is said to consist of machine learning (ML), large language models (LLM), natural language processing (NLP), generative AI (GenAI), robotics, knowledge-based systems (KBS), common-sense reasoning (CSR), etc. By using one or more of those techniques or technologies, you are presumably doing AI work or devising AI.

The fourth mainstay is a standout because it refers to the aspirations or seemingly ultimate goal of the AI field, aiming to attain AI that fully and convincingly exhibits intelligent behavior in a manner normally exhibited by humans. Not everyone necessarily agrees that this is the final goal of the AI field or that it is even a necessity underlying the crux of AI. In any case, the attainment of such an aspiration would suggest that a "true" AI system meets or exceeds the exhibited intelligence of humans. If the AI meets or is on par with the intelligence of humans we have achieved an amazing feat. On top of this, the belief is that we might be able to attain AI that exceeds the intelligence of humans and ergo be labeled as superhuman or exhibiting superintelligence.

Make a mental note of that fourth mainstay since we will be leaning into it when we get to discussing AGI.

The Neglected Or Omitted Confabulations

I'd like to briefly identify a host of other touchy subjects that come up when deeply thinking about what AI is. You are welcome to mull them over. Some are fastidiously philosophical.

All of these additional factors though are one way or another bound to have a material impact on what the definition of AI is said to be.

Here they are:

- (a) **Physical**. Does AI have to entail physicality or can AI be purely "intellectual"?
- (b) **Soul**. Does AI have to have a "soul" or can AI be considered attained even if lacking this?
- (c) **Sentience**. Does AI have to exhibit sentience in order to be considered true AI?
- (d) **Types**. What type of intelligence would AI have to exhibit such as brainiac style, emotional IQ, etc.?
- (e) **Levels**. What are the levels of intelligence that need to be exhibited?
- (f) **Animals**. Does animal intelligence count or is AI only with respect to the intelligence of humans?
- (g) **Wetware**. If the computer or machine is using or relying upon wetware does this negate being anointed as AI?
- Etc.

The Emergence Of The AGI Moniker

Congratulations for having slogged through the definitions and variations of what is meant by referring to AI. I had to take you through that murky territory in order to sensibly bring up the more recent moniker of Artificial General Intelligence or AGI.

The emergence of the AGI moniker is relatively straightforward and somewhat of a tale of woe.

First, back up in time. People were annoyingly using the AI moniker in ways that seemed to dilute the aspirational goal of the presumed definition. Just about any kind of software was being labeled as AI. The same can be said of today's systems. The immense popularity of the AI moniker has led many to eagerly slap the phrase onto anything that moves. Well, even things that don't move.

You could say that AI as a meaningly form of phraseology was getting watered down.

Any system that might have a mediocre amount of "AI" in it, despite not containing much of what we might call true AI, was nonetheless being touted as AI. This is something that people can get away with when there isn't an ironclad definition to hold their feet to the fire. It is extraordinarily difficult to police the use of the AI moniker when just about anyone can willy-nilly use the phrase in whatever way they so desire.

The marketing possibilities are endless.

That was one major concern about the vanilla-flavored AI phrase.

Another concern was that many AI systems were focused on specific tasks in a rather narrow fashion.

A superb AI-based chess-playing app could do only one thing, namely play chess. The same app could not tackle some other realm such as being able to play chess. Humans can play chess and readily learn to play checkers. It is easy-peasy. An AI app for chess playing was one-and-done. You could not readily alter the AI to do anything other than play great chess.

There was a grating feeling amongst AI researchers and AI developers that the watering down of the AI moniker and the narrowness of the prevailing AI systems was losing sight of the aspirational side of AI. We might entirely sub-optimize and not try to reach for the stars in terms of attaining true AI. True AI would presumably be AI that can exhibit intelligence on par with humans. This implies a kind of completeness encompassing generalizability. Humans can learn multiple things and switch from task to task. If AI is going to exhibit the intelligence of humans, we would be remiss to allow AI as a field of study to be reduced to being myopically narrow in what AI does.

What was to be done about this sticky situation?

You could try to get the entire planet to rethink what is meant by AI. I doubt that would be successful. The horse was already out of the barn.

Plus, sternly lecturing people that they are misusing the AI moniker would not get you very far. It would be irritating to those who got lectured and exhausting to those who had to continually render the lecture (you can hear the complaints, i.e., "those darned AI snobs are at it again!").

The more friction-free path would be to coin a new term. Yes, that's it, come up with a new phraseology that would convey the aspirational side of AI and overcome the tendency to plug away at AI that is disappointingly "only" narrow in scope (that's not to imply that narrow is somehow misguided, we can do a lot with narrow AI, including that narrow AI can seemingly get us to the broader AI too, hopefully).

The new name had to be catchy. If the phrase doesn't roll off the tongue or if it doesn't instantly convey the purpose, such a moniker will not be embraced or widely adopted. You could come up with something off the wall, but that wouldn't be pleasing. The notion would be to leverage the already popular AI moniker and do just enough to the wording to showcase that an additional direction was being taken.

Voila, Artificial General Intelligence, or AGI seems to fit that bill.

The abbreviation is spiffy and similar to the AI abbreviation. By merely adding one word into the middle of the expression you can ride on the coattails of the AI moniker. People will right away realize that something is afoot but still get the gist of things. Some might even think that you goofed and meant to say AI, perhaps accidentally inserting the word "general" into the composition. That's fine. Not everyone has to know what AGI is. Those in the know will know. Meanwhile, those not in the know will simply assume it is the same thing as AI or maybe a cousin of the AI moniker.

A wondrous solution to an AI insider disturbing problem.

For AI insiders, the inserted word "general" is intended to say volumes. It says that we need to go far beyond the narrow AI of the past and the present. We need to be able to devise AI that can do all manner of tasks and be as much a generalist as a specialist. AGI is what the aspirational side of AI is all about.

AI researchers who are pursuing an aspirational goal can therefore refer to their work as AI or refer to it as AGI, especially if they are undertaking the general path. I will soon be posting a column for example about the recent efforts of devising AI game-playing apps that can play a wide variety of games and learn on-the-fly to play new games that the AI hasn't encountered before. You could contend that this is along the lines of the AGI ambitions.

There is a downside to the AGI moniker. First, not everyone knows what it means. Second, we might once again experience a watering down. Suppose that people start to use AGI to refer to AI that is marginally of a generalized nature. This could eventually dominate the AGI realm. I suppose we might need to come up with yet another name to reboot or refocus things. Perhaps Artificial General General Intelligence (AGGI) or Artificial We-Really-Mean-It General Intelligence (AWRMIGI) might be floated as possibilities (that's a joke, so please laugh).

I've got a tough question for you.

Are you ready?

Do the prevailing definitions of AI, such as the ones I've provided at the earlier stage of this discussion, encompass AGI or do they somehow exclude AGI?

Some exhort that AGI is beyond the conventional moniker of AI. Others would claim that AGI is really within the framing of AI and we just don't happen to call it out or note things in that way. Once again, a definitional conundrum arises. A battle is being waged quietly about where AGI and AI either intersect or perhaps one is the subset of the other. It's sorrowfully messy.

Contemplate the permutations and combinations.

I began this discussion by suggesting that a succinct way to define AI is this:

- "AI is a system that exhibits intelligent behavior."

My go-to succinct way to define AGI is this:

- "AGI is a system that exhibits intelligent behavior of both a narrow and general manner on par with that of humans."

Notice that I got the narrow and general characteristics in there.

I also lifted the level of performance by stating that whatever intelligent behavior is exhibited is supposed to be on par with that of humans. Not all is well though. I realize this will create confusion for AGI which is superhuman since that would by definition be beyond the level of being on par with humans. We could add further wording or simply reserve the moniker of ASI (Artificial Superintelligence) for going beyond the AGI moniker. ASI is yet another floating moniker.

One especially troubling concern about the above succinct AGI definition is that it doesn't mention AI and therefore by omission begs (and leaves unanswered) the question of where this fits regarding AI all told. Yikes, more problems.

Here's another version that tries to deal with that:

- "AGI is an AI system that exhibits intelligent behavior of both a narrow and general manner on par with that of humans."

There are more controversies even about that slightly refined version. For example, if an AI researcher or AI developer comes up with an AGI that doesn't do anything special in a *narrow* way, but does exceedingly well in a *general* way, does that count as an AGI? Maybe the stated AGI definition would preclude such an instance.

It is tempting to drop out the narrow aspects altogether:

- "AGI is an AI system that exhibits intelligent behavior of a general manner on par with that of humans."

Unfortunately, the omission of the narrow element might get some upset because you could compellingly claim that people can do both, namely perform narrow things and do general things.

The omission of the word "narrow" perhaps suggests that AGI will only do generalized things and not be good at narrow things. Round and round this goes.

Semantically ambiguity is one of those darned if you do and darned if you don't type of irksome predicaments.

Perhaps we can try to work on better ways to define and articulate what is meant by AGI. Yes, we can, and that takes us to the next step of this hearty discussion.

Introduction To Levels Of Autonomy

In my above variations of the AGI moniker, there was an attempt to establish a level of performance. This is quite important.

I say that because the conventional definition of AI seems to be vague about the attainment of performance levels. To merely indicate that a system must exhibit intelligent behavior is wildly incomplete. Recall that I initially noted that we can readily carp about what is intelligent behavior and whether or not AI can be considered AI even if the AI is below the level of performance of humans.

If we stipulate that AGI must be on par with human-level performance this helps but can be a mighty hardship when devising AGI. You could come up with an AGI that is very impressive but not quite yet at a human level of performance. Should we chuck this AI system out of the AGI sphere, or can we allow it to remain there as a steppingstone toward greater and higher levels of performance?

One key aspect of performance consists of whether the AI or the AGI needs to have humans intellectually aiding the AI or AGI. As a rule of thumb, if the AI or AGI requires a human to perform some of the designated spheres of intelligence then we would be somewhat disappointed about the level of performance of the AI or AGI. Our highest aim is AI or AGI which is fully autonomous. No human is needed for the AI or AGI to do whatever it does.

This does not preclude the AI or AGI from interacting with humans. Please keep that notably in mind.

We are likely going to want the AI or AGI to indeed interact with humans. The thing is, the AI or AGI should not be dependent upon humans to do the heavy intellectual lifting. That is supposed to be the prevue of the AI or AGI.

For example, you decide to access an AI or AGI that is able to exhibit intelligent behavior in the medical field and can do so on par with a seasoned medical doctor. You aren't supposed to be the one bringing medical knowledge to the table. That's what the AI or AGI is supposed to be doing. At the same time, we would naturally expect that the AI or AGI would interact with you to determine your symptoms and seek a diagnosis of your ailment. Furthermore, it could be that you too are a medical doctor and therefore want to confer with the AI or AGI on a doctor-to-doctor basis.

There is already a field of endeavor that leverages the notion of autonomy and is a realm that you probably already have heard about. I am referring to autonomous vehicles (AVs) such as self-driving cars.

Let's briefly touch upon the conventional levels of autonomy (LoA) as specified for AVs.

There is a handy dandy standard developed by the SAE (Society for Automotive Engineers) that lays out a set of six levels of autonomy, ranging from a numbering of zero to a top level of five. Most people assume that the standard LoA is only intended for self-driving cars. Nope, it is a broad framework that was devised to intentionally be reused in other domains.

The topmost level of five is considered a fully autonomous agent, such as a self-driving car that can drive by itself in whatever situation a human driver could do so. The idea is that a self-driving car at Level 5 is an AV that must be able to perform the driving task without needing a human driver at the wheel. Level 4 is similar, but the autonomous capability is only within an identified ODD (operational design domain). For example, a self-driving car at Level 4 might be set up to drive in San Francisco but cannot safely drive when in another domain such as Los Angeles or Chicago. The levels below the fourth level are pretty much circumstances involving the need for a human driver to be at the wheel.

I have reviewed and at times commented that one weakness of the SAE standard is that the topmost level of a five refers to human capacities. My beef is that there should be an additional level above the existing topmost. This added level would encompass the use case of superhuman capabilities. When considering levels of autonomy, we should account for the possibility of being able to devise AI or AGI that is "superhuman" and able to exceed humans. I would argue that a Level 6 encompassing "superhuman" autonomy would be helpful and bring the number of levels up to a total of seven (I've used that self-adjusted scale in various of my AI research frameworks).

You are now up-to-speed about levels of autonomy and we are ready for tying this into the definitions of AI and AGI.

Google DeepMind Makes A Proposal About AGI

I am going to walk you through an intriguing and notable proposal about AGI that was authored by AI researchers at Google DeepMind and recently posted online. I will be quoting from the paper entitled "Levels of AGI: Operationalizing Progress on the Path to AGI" by Meredith Ringel Morris, Jascha Sohl-Dickstein, Noah Fiedel, Tris Warkentin, Allan Dafoe, Aleksandra Faust, Clement Farabet, and Shane Legg, which was posted online by Google DeepMind on November 4, 2023. I urge you to consider reading the full paper if this is a topic of keen interest to you.

One of my favorite quotes from the paper is this one and demonstratively echoes my discussion herein about how the contemporary definitions of AGI are all over the map:

- "However, if you were to ask 100 AI experts to define what they mean by 'AGI,' you would likely get 100 related but different definitions."

They nailed it.

Now that we agree on the problem at hand, let's see what they propose to do about the vexing situation.

Here is their proposal:

- "We propose a framework for classifying the capabilities and behavior of Artificial General Intelligence (AGI) models and their precursors. This framework introduces levels of AGI performance, generality, and autonomy. It is our hope that this framework will be useful in an analogous way to the levels of autonomous driving, by providing a common language to compare models, assess risks, and measure progress along the path to AGI."

Aha, as you can plainly see, they propose that we can beneficially clarify the nature of AGI by utilizing levels of autonomy. That's why I sneakily dragged you through the discussion about LoA for AVs and self-driving cars. Had to get you ready for this big reveal.

I had already noted that having tighter definitions for things is useful for a wide variety of sensible and crucial reasons. They point out that for AGI there are immensely bona fide reasons and payoffs from more sufficiently specifying what AGI is:

- "Shared operationalizable definitions for these concepts will support: comparisons between models; risk assessments and mitigation strategies; clear criteria from policymakers and regulators; identifying goals, predictions, and risks for research and development; and the ability to understand and communicate where we are along the path to AGI."

Moving on, I liked that they opted to examine the numerous competing approaches that purport to aid in clarifying what AI and AGI consist of. I've covered the Turing Test many times, which has become the conventional means of trying to figure out whether true AI has been attained or not. The problem is that the Turing Test has various twists and turns that tend to make it not quite as foolproof as we might all desire.

In their paper, they briefly touch up these nine conventional attempts at trying to ascertain true AI:

- Case Study 1: The Turing Test.
- Case Study 2: Strong AI – Systems Possessing Consciousness.
- Case Study 3: Analogies to the Human Brain
- Case Study 4: Human-Level Performance on Cognitive Tasks
- Case Study 5: Ability to Learn Tasks
- Case Study 6: Economically Valuable Work
- Case Study 7: Flexible and General – The 'Coffee Test' and Related Challenges.
- Case Study 8: Artificial Capable Intelligence.
- Case Study 9: SOTA LLMs as Generalists.

You might opt to take a look at the paper if those are facets that you aren't familiar with, or that you kind of know but hadn't thought about why they have various fractures and rough edges to them. I won't repeat the details of those facets here. You can find them covered across many of my columns and if reader interest arises, I'll be happy to do a dedicated column posting about those in one place at one time. Happy to oblige.

Another important consideration to get in front of people is to lay out what type of criteria or characteristics we all should be thinking about when it comes to defining true AI, namely AGI. The paper covers these six criteria:

- Criteria #1: Focus on Capabilities, not Processes.
- Criteria #2: Focus on Generality and Performance.
- Criteria #3: Focus on Cognitive and Metacognitive Tasks.
- Criteria #4: Focus on Potential, not Deployment.
- Criteria #5: Focus on Ecological Validity.
- Criteria #6: Focus on the Path to AGI, not a Single Endpoint.

On a bottom-line oriented excerpt, they bring up these erstwhile considerations underlying defining AGI:

- "What is the set of tasks that constitute the generality criteria? What proportion of such tasks must an AI system master to achieve a given level of generality in our schema? Are there some tasks that must always be performed to meet the criteria for certain generality levels, such as metacognitive tasks?"

In case you were anticipating a benchmark that could be used to gauge whether a particular system has reached AGI or ascertain what level it has attained, the paper notes that more work needs to be done on deriving benchmarks (thus, I hope you will be inspired to pursue such efforts, so please put this on your list of things to do, thanks):

- "Because of the immense complexity of this process, as well as the importance of including a wide range of perspectives (including cross-organizational and multi-disciplinary viewpoints), we do not propose a benchmark in this paper. Instead, we work to clarify the ontology a benchmark should attempt to measure. We also discuss properties an AGI benchmark should possess."

I believe that gives you an overall sense of the landscape of the paper. We can now dive into the proposed levels of autonomy.

Please know that my herein recap won't do full justice to the nuances. I aim to whet your palette. Here goes.

The Levels of Autonomy Proposed For AGI

First, as you now are assuredly aware, one big complication is the issue of narrow versus general. The proposed approach says that we ought to encompass both of those factors. We can thus appropriately stipulate that for each level of the levels of autonomy, there will be both an allied category for the narrow AI and a side-by-side allied category for the general AI. This escapes the usual dilemma of being only narrow-oriented or only general-oriented.

We can have our cake and eat it too.

Second, the number of levels will be six, thus somewhat akin to the SAE standard that I mentioned. Numbering will again start with zero and go to five.

As a side note, many people complain that the SAE standard doesn't count from a starting point of 1, which would seem easier since the topmost number would be six and ergo match the notion that there are six levels.

All I can say is that computer people love to start numbering with the number zero. Furthermore, you could persuasively argue that zero immediately suggests an absence of autonomy, while if the numbering started with a one you might be tempted to assume that there is some semblance of autonomy at the starting point of things. See, it almost does make sense.

Back to our main focus. The topmost level is going to differ from the SAE standard by denoting that Level 5 is considered superhuman. This nicely aligns with my earlier point about trying to ensure that a superhuman category ought to be encompassed in a LoA. I'm sure that some might argue that there should be an added Level 6 that would be superhuman. Doing so would more neatly align with the SAE standard of having six base levels (absent of superhuman). Anyway, these are debates worth considering and there are tradeoffs as to how many levels you devise and what each level constitutes.

Another key consideration is what name you give to each level.

The typical idea is that you should just refer to the levels by their respective numbers. That is hard for some people to readily grasp and remember. As such, it is useful to give a word that conveys what the level constitutes. The downside is that the word might be misleading or only a rough guide. Words have semantic ambiguity, as I've noted several times. A number for a level is a number. Anyway, if you want a LoA to catch on, you usually have to painfully come up with words that designate what each level represents and then live with it (or change the wording if the wording gets lambasted or doesn't take hold).

Here then are the six levels laid out in the paper:

- Level 0: **No AI**
- Level 1: **Emerging** (equal to or somewhat better than an unskilled human)
- Level 2: **Competent** (at least 50th percentile of skilled adults)
- Level 3: **Expert** (at least 90th percentile of skilled adults)
- Level 4: **Virtuoso** (at least 99th percentile of skilled adults)
- Level 5: **Superhuman** (outperforms 100% of humans)

The parenthetical portions are noteworthy.

Here's why.

If I tell you that an AI or AGI can perform on par with humans, a smarmy but suitable retort is to ask which humans you are referring to. Not all humans are the same. Some humans are better at some things than others. If I tell you that I have a superb AI-infused chess-playing app, and I further claim it can beat humans in chess, the question arises as to which humans I am referring to. All humans? Or, maybe the world's top chess players can at times win over the AI. In that case, perhaps 99.999% of humans on Earth can be beaten by the AI in chess. Still, there is that small segment of humans that can potentially win.

Take a look at how the paper divides up the percentiles of humans. There is ample room for discussion and debate about those percentiles. That's fine and we can expect that such a strawman will get the creative juices going so that we can collect further input on the stratification approaches and their tradeoffs.

I will next show you the overlay of the respective narrow category and the respective general category. The paper shows this as a spreadsheet grid which is easier to visually explore.

Overlay of the proposed levels of AGI autonomy with the narrow component:

- Level 0: No AI – **Narrow Non-AI** (e.g., calculator app)
- Level 1: Emerging - **Narrow AI** (e.g., rules-based systems)
- Level 2: Competent – **Narrow AI** (e.g., Siri, Alexa)
- Level 3: Expert – **Narrow AI** (e.g., Dall-E 2)
- Level 4: Virtuoso – **Narrow AI** (e.g., AlphaGo)
- Level 5: Superhuman – **Narrow AI** (e.g., AlphaFold)

The proposed levels of AGI autonomy with the general component:

- Level 0: No AI – **General Non-AI** (e.g., Amazon Mechanical Turk)
- Level 1: Emerging - **General AGI** (e.g., ChatGPT, Bard, Llama 2)
- Level 2: Competent – **General AGI** (not yet achieved)
- Level 3: Expert – **General AGI** (not yet achieved)
- Level 4: Virtuoso – **General AGI (**not yet achieved)
- Level 5: Superhuman – **General AGI** (aka ASI or Artificial Superintelligence, not yet achieved)

The overlay showing the narrow component has a list of examples that the paper highlighted to showcase what the level is said to encompass. Doing so was a nice touch to make the levels more tangibly comprehensible. For example, they list Siri and Alex as Level 2 in the narrow AI category, which then gives you an immediate sense of what Level 2 in narrow encompasses. The famous AlphaGo is listed as an example of the narrow AI category of Level 4. And so on.

The overly for the general component of the proposed LoA also includes some examples. According to the paper, the assertion is made that for Level 2 and higher there aren't any AGI examples today in the general component. This seems to make sense. Whether Level 1 suitably lists some of today's generative AI apps is something I'm sure will cause heartburn for some, while others might believe that Level 1 is an apt spot or even try to contend that a Level 2 would be suitable too. There is plenty here to get AI insider's blood boiling.

I would politely ask that blood boiling not be undertaken.

Whatever you do, do not judge the levels by the examples. This would be akin to letting the tail wag the dog. The focus should be on the levels. Whether we agree on which of the various example AI apps fit in this or that level is not especially consequential at this stage. Let's get the keystone fundamentals figured out and we can always move around the examples as needed.

Kudos to DeepMind for their proposal and for helping to get the ball rolling on adding levels of autonomy to what is meant by AGI and also covering a slew of additional vital considerations that are well worth giving due attention for formulating AGI definitionally.

Conclusion

You now have the skinny on AI and AGI in terms of the terms and where things sit today. Welcome to the AI insider club. You are ready to do your part. As you can see, we are just beginning to figure out what AGI is. The proposal that I covered provides a useful strawman and showcases a taste of what is involved. The world is ready to further the pursuit of defining AGI. Likewise, we have a lot of work to do on defining AI.

CHAPTER 2
AGI AND UNIVERSAL NATURAL LANGUAGE

In this chapter, I examine an intriguing speculation that once we advance AI to become AGI (artificial general intelligence), doing so will spur AGI to devise a new universal natural language for humanity to adopt, which then radically reshapes how we think and act. It is definitely an outside-the-box proposition and deserves a moment of keen reflection.

Language Shapes Our Thinking

Let's mull over the role of natural languages in our daily existence.

I'm sure you've heard or read that natural languages tend to shape our thinking processes. The idea is that whatever language you happen to know impacts what you are able to think about and how you process mental considerations. The classic example is the claim that Eskimos have a multitude of words to represent ice and snow. This in turn enables them to think about ice and snow in ways that others lacking those words might not conceivably do.

This strident belief that languages shape our thinking is referred to as the linguistic relativity hypothesis, which is also informally known as Whorfianism.

There is a bit of controversy associated with whether the claim about the language of Eskimos is fully accurate on this matter, but the crux is that languages being able to shape our thinking seems intuitively sensible and logical. If you meet someone who doesn't know a particular word, you've probably had a difficult time conversing on the topic at hand.

You might have to figure out other ways to express the matter. They could lack an entire semblance of a concept or aspect of life that hasn't yet dawned on them, partially since their language doesn't express the matter or they've not encountered an equivalence in their language.

Devising A Universal Natural Language

Imagine that you could develop from scratch a new natural language that humans might find useful to adopt.

This somewhat happened back in 1887 when Leyzer Zamenhof created a new natural language called Esperanto. He hoped to have everyone adopt a new language that would cause people to feel more connected with each other and readily able to communicate with each other. The United Nations many years later in 2017 noted his support for intercultural dialogue and around that time an estimated 2 million people were speaking Esperanto. That's obviously a drop in the bucket when you consider there are around 8 billion people on Earth, but it's kind of amazing to realize that some people still embrace his devised language.

It is an uphill battle to get people to switch over to a brand-new language. First of all, if not many other people speak the language, why should you use your time and energy to learn it? Very few others would be able to interact with you in that language. Worse still, maybe the language will ultimately fizzle out and you'll be left with a dead language in your head that doesn't seem to do you much good.

Another qualm would be that the language might not express things that you already know, versus based on whatever other languages you are fluent in. It would be exasperating to learn another language and feel jammed up that you cannot fully express yourself. You would tend to revert to the languages you already have squarely in hand.

All in all, a brand-new language would have to possess some really compelling facilities to get people to avidly adopt the language.

AGI Enters Into The Big Picture

You are ready now for the big reveal on this mind-bending topic.

Suppose we advance AI to become AGI. AGI then looks around and decides that the prevailing natural languages that humans have devised are not as robust and insightful as they could be. Humans have merely stepwise crafted new languages and have never completely been willing to give a shot at crafting a language out of the blue that would essentially be the pinnacle of all feasible languages.

To clarify, this wouldn't be an exercise in simply coming up with a new language for the heck of it. There would be a grand purpose involved. The brand-new language would be intended to foster thinking in humans that is beyond our conventional thinking. Human-devised natural languages are holding us back. We don't realize this. Meanwhile, AGI does realize this.

So, AGI opts to create a new natural language for us. The AGI is doing what it can to aid humankind and further our intellectual progress. Happy face.

Humans Love Or Fear This

One potential reaction by humankind is that we don't want a brand-new language. We are perfectly fine with the languages we already have. A new language would be burdensome. The effort to learn the language and put it into everyday use would require a lot of human time and cost. We pat AGI on the head and say thanks, but no thanks.

Some might also be highly suspicious of the new language.

The worry goes like this. Maybe AGI wants to have ultimate mind control over humans. A sneaky and clever way to do this would be to saddle us with a language that the AGI somehow can manipulate to its advantage. If we all adopt the language, it could be a massive trap.

The AGI has now got us right where it wants us. Sad face.

You can bet your bottom dollar that a huge amount of scrutiny would go into inspecting the brand-new language. Governments might warn to avoid learning the language until the needed assessments have been completed. Others would undoubtedly rush to learn the language, despite any warnings by authorities, since the assumption is that knowing another language can't really hurt anyone.

A notable concern would be raised about the possibility of babies learning this brand-new language, doing so before they've learned a tried-and-true human-devised natural language. In other words, suppose a baby in a household that speaks only English is first introduced to this new language before they are versed in English.

Could this alter their thinking processes and if so, would that alteration have a lifelong impact, and be a good thing or be a disaster for them?

George Orwell said it best: "But if thought corrupts language, language can also corrupt thought."

AGI Defends The Language

Presumably, AGI would outrightly indicate why humanity is going to greatly benefit by adopting the new language. In an Eskimo language aspect analogous way, the AGI might explain that if we learn the new language, we will have a vocabulary that will expand our existing way of thinking. Doing so will put us on an even playing field with AGI.

Perhaps breakthrough discoveries and inventions will be much more likely by humanity due to humans adopting the new language. Peace on Earth might be more probable because everyone speaks the same language and has the same collective understanding. It is like Esperanto on steroids and fully backed by the already impressive AGI.

Consider the rollout aspects.

At first, nearly everyone who learns this brand-new language would be doing so as a second language (or third, fourth, etc., depending on how many languages someone already knows).

The world isn't going to suddenly change over to a new language in the blink of an eye. People would be speaking their other tongues and also using the newly crafted language.

Eventually, assuming that the new language is truly that powerful and beneficial, the expectation would be that all other natural languages would fade out. Scholars would keep those languages around merely for historical purposes. Nearly 100% of the world would be using the new language and rarely ever resort to one of the then-considered retired languages.

Structure Of The Language

What would such a brand-new language look like?

One viewpoint is that the language would have to resemble the natural languages that we already know. This would make it easier to adopt and a lot less challenging to learn. If the new language consisted of some strange-looking concoction, perhaps all numerical in its substance, it seems doubtful that widespread adoption could take place. People just wouldn't be able to grasp it.

We also need to consider how the language works in both written form and when spoken aloud. Imagine for example that the new language was easy to write down but extremely hard to use via the spoken word. That's a problem. Getting the language to be widely adopted would have to appease both the writing aspects and the speaking aspects.

AGI is faced with quite a tough puzzle. The new language must generally conform to existing or known natural languages if it is going to be widely accepted. Meanwhile, the new language is supposed to have a compelling basis for adoption, such as expanding our minds and reshaping our thinking processes.

It is a tall order, that's for sure.

A contrarian perspective is that it would be fine if the brand-new language was hard to adopt. Even if the language doesn't resemble our existing languages, no worries, since humans are adaptable and would adapt to this new language.

The key is whether overcoming the barriers to learning the language was worth the benefits that would accrue.

What We Gain And We Lose

Contemplate the impact that having a universal natural language might have on human customs and culture. Some dread the idea that this would almost inevitably neutralize our differences and make us entirely homogenous. Everyone speaking and using the same language would potentially lead to a unitary way of thinking and acting.

It is almost as though we have become staid robots.

Not everyone believes in that doom-and-gloom outcome. Perhaps we could still retain culture and customs, even if using the same across-the-board language. There isn't an axiomatic reason that we must be the same merely due to using the same language.

One of the most exciting aspects of the brand-new language is that it might portend a kind of tipping point for human cognition. This can be likened to a linguistic singularity, whereby humankind demonstrably leaps forward in our intellectual prowess. This is done without having to do implants into our brains. Nor do we need to wait thousands of years for evolution to gradually adjust our noggins.

For now, I'll give the last word on this hefty topic to Nathaniel Hawthorne: "Words -- so innocent and powerless as they are, as standing in a dictionary, how potent for good and evil they become in the hands of one who knows how to combine them."

Will we accept an AGI-devised language? Then again, maybe we will implore AGI to devise a new language and open Pandora's box of our own volition.

CHAPTER 3

AGI IS MORE THAN NORMAL TECH

In this chapter, I examine a rapidly expanding controversy that AI is nothing more than just normal technology. The proposition goes like this. We are overstating the underlying nature and impact of AI and allowing ourselves to be deluded into a false sense of AI as superhuman. This causes us to then fail to suitably deal with conventional AI and become hopelessly mired in fanciful daydreams of what AI might someday become. Ergo, let's recalibrate our mindset and view AI as normal technology. Period, end of story.

The AI community is quite strongly divided on both sides of this assertion. Some heartily insist that it is about time that the emperor with no clothes was finally revealed, while others vehemently disagree with the idea that AI is merely normal technology.

AI As Normal Technology

An intriguing question arises about the status of conventional AI.

Is conventional AI merely the same as other "normal" technologies, such as on par with the Internet or electricity?

Observe that the comparison of AI is being made to tremendous and transformative technologies including the advent of the Internet and the discovery and harnessing of electricity.

The point is that the word "normal" should be level-set as outsized tech that has been wholly disruptive and a huge change to how humankind operates. Do not fall into the mental trap of construing the word "normal" as meaning akin to a normal toaster or a normal mousetrap.

Mull over whether you believe that AI is normal or exceedingly extraordinary.

The Case For AI As Normal Tech

Assume for the sake of discussion that you or someone you know is on the side of believing that AI is normal technology.

How can anyone arrive at that conclusion?

One perspective is that conventional AI is running on everyday computer servers, uses everyday aspects of inputs and outputs, and employs cleverly devised algorithms but all of this is well within human craftsmanship. It is all still bits and bytes. There aren't any magical incantations involved. No voodoo.

Yet many seem to have turned the public perception of contemporary AI into a hullabaloo, maybe even into a farce. Some AI insiders have contributed to this sense of otherworldly aura by insisting that they see "sparks" of sentience and consciousness in generative AI and large language models (LLMs). Sorry to say, those grandiose visions have been debunked.

Hard-nosed AI insiders who are fed up with the fakery and over-the-top proclamations about modern-era AI are declaring that enough is enough. It is time to draw a line in the sand. Set aside all this nonsense about AI that walks on water and leaps tall buildings in a single bound.

Drawing A Line In The Sand

A recently posted paper on April 15, 2025, entitled "AI as Normal Technology" which was co-authored by researchers Arvind Narayanan and Sayash Kapoor, doing so under the auspices of Columbia University and their Knight First Amendment Institute, made these salient points (excerpts):

- "We articulate a vision of artificial intelligence (AI) as normal technology. To view AI as normal is not to understate its impact—even transformative, general-purpose technologies such as electricity and the internet are "normal" in our conception."

- "But it is in contrast to both utopian and dystopian visions of the future of AI which have a common tendency to treat it akin to a separate species, a highly autonomous, potentially superintelligent entity."

- "The statement "AI is normal technology" is three things: a description of current AI, a prediction about the foreseeable future of AI, and a prescription about how we should treat it. "

- "We view AI as a tool that we can and should remain in control of, and we argue that this goal does not require drastic policy interventions or technical breakthroughs. We do not think that viewing AI as a humanlike intelligence is currently accurate or useful for understanding its societal impacts, nor is it likely to be in our vision of the future."

Boom, drop the mic.

Their viewpoint has stirred a hornet's nest. If you are someone who ardently believes that all the zany headlines stirring the fearmongering, gaslighting, and breathless existential risks of AI have got to come to a halt, you are likely to embrace and applaud the contention that AI is normal technology. Others would disagree with the contention and assert that this is nothing more than a form of gaslighting about the alleged gaslighting about AI.

As an aside, the paper goes into great detail about their rationale that AI is a normal technology and you might consider reading the full paper if this is a matter of direct interest to you.

The Complacency Danger

One worry about conceiving AI as normal technology is that this might slide society into a semblance of complacency about AI.

Allow me to briefly elaborate on this. Right now, the talk of AI as possibly being able to cure cancer and meanwhile that AI might wipe out humanity provides a potent focus on what AI is and where AI is headed. Sure, maybe it is hyperbole, but the only way to get society to be attentive often necessitates going over the top.

If we all agree to henceforth say that AI is normal technology, perhaps AI will no longer garner headlines and no longer gain the attention of policymakers, regulators, and other such stakeholders. We will relegate AI to the realm of the techies. Looming societal impacts will undoubtedly be unexplored since AI techies either aren't thinking about those heady matters or assume that it will all get figured out once AI emerges once again into the global consciousness.

That could be like letting the horse out of the barn. You could have kept the horse in the barn or at least prepared to smartly release the horse, but instead, you kept your head deeply buried in the sand (two metaphors for the price of one).

The Case For Abnormal Impacts

There is another twist on why the premise that AI is normal technology seems worrisome.

First, let's go ahead and place the matter of AGI and ASI completely outside our purview. Just go along with the supposition that AGI and ASI are not in the picture. Only conventional AI as we know it today is inside the big picture.

One argument is that the impacts of even conventional AI are, in a sense, abnormal. You can proceed to assume that AI is a normal technology, but the societal impacts go beyond those of other normal technologies. The impacts are abnormal.

There are normal technologies that lead to normal impacts. That's fine.

The thing is, there are normal technologies that lead to abnormal impacts. Lumping AI into the normal technology's classification can falsely lead to thinking that AI has just normal impacts.

Foreseeable Futures That Miss The Mark

In the excerpted points regarding the propositional case of AI as a normal technology, some inquisitors have noted a make-or-break assertion in there. The deal is this. The premise includes a crucial underpinning about predicting the foreseeable future of AI (note: I have italicized that portion here so you can readily observe it here):

- "The statement 'AI is normal technology' is three things: a description of current AI, *a prediction about the foreseeable future of AI*, and a prescription about how we should treat it" (ibid).

Well, throughout history there have been numerous instances of predictions concerning so-called foreseeable futures that were significantly off base. The upshot is that the foreseeable future for conventional AI could be that we continue to bump along and see modest advances that aren't especially surprising. Same old, same old. If that's the case, the normalcy of the said-to-be normal technology of AI retains its normalcy.

But if we advance AI more demonstrably, doing so within the foreseeable future, the potential for AI to go far beyond conventional human control might catch us by surprise.

Think of it this way. Imagine we all agreed to treat conventional AI as a normal technology and applied normal scrutiny accordingly. Then, seemingly out of the blue, and breaking our assumptions about the foreseeable future, AI suddenly gets bigger than we can handle.

Betting heavily on the presumed *foreseeable future* of AI might be quite a gamble.

Undercutting Of Drastic Interventions

There has also been heartburn about the lay-low aspects of nullifying a willingness or readiness to employ potential drastic interventions associated with conventional AI. As noted in one of the excerpted points (portion italicized here for ease of visualization):

- "We view AI as a tool that we can and should remain in control of, and we argue that this goal *does not require drastic policy interventions* or technical breakthroughs" (ibid).

If we establish a mindset that no drastic policy interventions will be needed, do we undercut the chances of spotting a need for drastic interventions and thus delay or fail to identify and adopt such interventions on a timely basis?

Perhaps conventional AI gets infused into critical systems that we all rely upon for daily existence and survival. The AI placed into that posture puts us at risk. It could be that we need to perform some form of drastic policy intervention. But the normal technology perspective possibly has convinced us that nothing drastic is needed and that otherwise conventional interventions will suffice.

Predictions Of AGI On The Horizon

Related to the matter of the foreseeable future of AI, there are a multitude of AI luminary predictions that AGI will be attained in the near term such as 2027 to 2030, and surveys of AI specialists have generally suggested that 2040 is a considered "almost certainly by then" AGI date.

Do you consider 2027 to 2030 as within the rubric of a foreseeable future or is it outside that range?

In other words, many in the AI community believe that we are either just a few years away from AGI or at most about a dozen or so years away. You can certainly disagree with those predictions. Many do. Others believe in those dates fiercely.

The trouble goes this way. AGI would have such an enormous consequential impact that we cannot sensibly lump AGI into the conventional AI bucket. And to clarify, we are stipulating that AGI is not superhuman, and "only" on par with human intellect. This sets aside the superhuman AI conflating.

Thoughts On The Normalcy Debate

It sure would be nice if we could have our cake and eat it too. The circumstances would be that we could keep two fundamental dimensions in our heads at the same time, in a balanced effort:

- (1) We construe conventional AI as considered "normal technology" and do so in a strictly kind of unpolluted status -- keeping at arm's length those grand schemes of AI that become AGI or ASI.

- (2) Meanwhile, we still entertain the possibility of attaining AGI (or possibly ASI) and anticipate and prepare for that possibility, but not to the extent that we overinflate the first point and get mired in failing to focus suitably on conventional AI (the "normal technology").

Can we do that?

It's an exceedingly extraordinarily challenging non-normal task.

CHAPTER 4
AI MAKERS MUST BOND TO MAKE AGI

In this chapter, I examine an ongoing heated debate on whether the prevailing approach of independent AI makers striving mightily on their own to attain artificial general intelligence (AGI) and artificial superintelligence (ASI) is a feasible strategy. It might be that the prevailing Lone Ranger pathway will not get us all the way to the vaunted AGI or ASI.

Some assert that it takes a village to arrive at the pinnacle of AI. A kumbaya or all-together-now mindset might be the only fruitful course of action. Share and share alike.

The Lone Ranger Path To Pinnacle AI

Imagine that we can arrive at AGI or ASI. No one knows for sure if we can, but let's assume that by hook or crook, we will arrive there.

The prevailing route right now is that AI makers are striving mightily to each independently arrive at such pinnacle AI. This makes abundant sense when you consider the pot of gold and the incredible fame that will be imbued upon the first AI maker that reaches the pinnacle of AI.

Fame and fortune are going to be aplenty.

The major AI vendors often treat their AI wares with the utmost semblance of intellectual property (IP) propriety. They keep the inner mechanisms of their budding AI as a deep secret.

The idea is that their investment in AI is based on a belief that the best approach entails a do-it-themselves conception. Fierce competition exists. Ongoing efforts are afoot to create moats or enact barriers to prevent their competitors from copying their distinct accomplishments.

Just to give you a heads-up about this secrecy qualm, there are already grave worries that by not revealing the inner facets, the AI makers are going to be hiding immense safety and security issues that no one knows exist. The AI makers might not have sufficiently performed due diligence to figure out where there are bugs and problems in their respective AIs. Meanwhile, the outside world has no means to poke into the AI to ferret out those maladies.

The possibility of hidden troubles and vulnerabilities is troubling and puts us all at .

Some might immediately claim that the open-source movement in AI negates these secrecy qualms, but even the open-source adherents often leave out key aspects such as what data they used to data-train their AI.

The crux is that we are heading toward pinnacle AI that is primarily independently devised and not being pursued on an across-the-board team-oriented basis per se. It is worth noting that there have been repeated calls for a Manhattan Project of sorts, akin to how the atomic bomb was invented.

The idea would be to bring together on a national basis the disparate AI efforts. Their goal would be to attain ASI or AGI. So far, such clamor for a coordinated collaborative endeavor of that magnitude has not materialized.

Why Rugged Individualism Won't Work

Let's unpack the case that rugged individualism isn't going to cut the mustard.

Here are the topmost five reasons that a solo AI maker isn't presumably going to reach pinnacle AI:

- **(1) Complexity of the AI challenge**. Reaching the pinnacle of AI is an immense challenge that no single AI maker can successfully pull off. There are too many breakthroughs needed. There are too many allied domains requiring expertise. Even the largest AI makers and high-tech behemoths don't have that number and depth of labor resources.

- **(2) Lack of AI safety and AI-human alignment**. Aiming at pinnacle AI might be reachable in its barest sense, but the odds are it won't have sufficient safety and controls if a single AI maker alone is doing the work. You see, an AI maker is bound to cut corners in their desperate zeal to declare they have AGI or ASI in their midst. We can't let unfettered uncontrolled AGI or ASI be attained simply for the glory of an AI maker.

- **(3) Insufficient AI computational resources**. Besides mental prowess and labor resources, another issue is that the volume and nature of the computational resources required will be beyond the budget of a single AI maker. Big iron is needed to achieve AGI or ASI. Really big iron. Gigantic.

- **(4) Reinventing the AI wheel repeatedly.** When AI makers work independently, they are going to repeat the same mistakes that others have already addressed but have equally kept secret from everyone else. Progress is costlier and less likely to reach the end goal accordingly. Lots of dead ends will be encountered over and over.

- **(5) Worries about who calls the AI shots.** Pinnacle AI will have profound societal impacts. Do we really want a single AI maker to decide who gets to use AGI or ASI? Suppose the AI maker uses it to overturn the government or undertake evildoer endeavors. Thus, we must prevent a solo AI maker from getting to pinnacle AI even if they can do so, for the sake of society all told.

Those reasons are a combination of the infeasibility of an AI maker to attain pinnacle AI, along with concerns about why we wouldn't want a single AI maker to get there on their own.

Why Rugged Individualism Will Work

You might guess that not everyone agrees with the sentiment that the individualized approach is all bad.

The five frequently noted counterarguments include these salient points:

- **(1) Competitiveness fuels AI innovation.** The only way we will get to pinnacle AI is via the juices of competition. If you force out competition or even if AI makers agree to wholly cooperate, the undercutting of competitive spirit will ruin the pursuit. Allow the battle of wits to churn forward with AI makers striving against each other, and AGI or ASI will be devised.

- **(2) Divergent approaches to AI will avoid ruts.** Promoting creativity and divergence of AI methods toward attaining pinnacle AI is the best strategy right now since no one can say what the needed path consists of. Binding together AI makers or undertaking the effort via some government umbrella is going to drive us into a rut. New ideas will be squelched. Conformity will be king. We might never see pinnacle AI due to working as lemmings.

- **(3) Sharing on AI is already plentiful.** It is a misnomer to contend that AI makers are individualistic. AI scientists routinely move from one AI maker to the other. Research is publicly posted and shared. AI development tools are crafted and made widely available. AI makers are already cooperating and collaborating, though it might seem hidden from plain view.

- **(4) Avoidance of stifling bureaucracy.** Nearly any large-scale collaborative approach to attain pinnacle AI would get bogged down by bureaucracy, be consumed by needless infighting, wrestling with disputed agendas, and the like. Solo AI makers might have their internal bureaucracies to contend with, but that's a far cry from some overcontrolling mega-bureaucracy that would kill the goose before it lays the golden egg.

- **(5) Spreads out the chances of AI success.** Since we do not know what is going to get us to pinnacle AI, our wisest bet would be to pursue all angles. This improves the chances of success. As they say, putting all your eggs in only one basket is a heightened vulnerability.

Those points are considered the other side of the coin in this acrid debate.

Many Dimensions To Be Considered

Where do you stand on the issue at hand?

Cogent and convincing arguments persist on both sides.

Geopolitical dynamics also enter the picture. Suppose for example one nation opts for the individualistic bent, while a different nation goes the teamwork route. If the teamwork nation prevails and attains pinnacle AI, the one that pursued the individualistic approach will be left high and dry.

The thing is, you can make the reverse case as a viable claim too, namely that what if the individualistic nation prevails and the teamwork nation doesn't?

Some final thoughts for now on this evolving and hotly debated topic.

Regardless of whether the individualistic versus teamwork route is selected, we need to earnestly and with great vigor continue and expand the pursuit of AI alignment with human values. The hope is to either design and build AI such that pinnacle AI will be human value aligned or that we've done enough so that pinnacle AI itself will be able to extrapolate and model on those precepts.

A fitting quote to conclude with is this famous line by Abraham Lincoln: "The most reliable way to predict the future is to create it." That's the mode we are in for attaining pinnacle AI and the question is, are we on the right road?

Time will tell.

CHAPTER 5
SLOW ROLL TO AGI AND ASI

In this chapter, I do some myth-busting by taking apart a prevailing assumption that attaining artificial general intelligence (AGI) and artificial superintelligence (ASI) will of necessity happen on a spontaneous basis. The prevailing wisdom is that AGI or ASI will just suddenly and miraculously be reached, as though a spark of lightning suddenly made it happen.

A counter viewpoint is that we are going to stepwise incrementally make our way to the topmost AI. A gradual but persistent slow roll is an alternative viable means of landing on AGI or ASI.

The AI Big Bang Theory

One of the most enduring theories in the AI field has been that the attainment of AGI or ASI will involve a kind of AI Big Bang, namely that a sudden instantaneous intelligence explosion will cause conventional AI to rapidly expand into pinnacle AI. Some refer to this as the big rush, another is that it is the AI foom or flourish, and another coined terminology is that the awe-inspiring moment of said-to-be "AI singularity" will occur.

The idea is that for whatever reasons one might conjure, a bubbling brew of AI intelligence will intensely heat up and in so doing reach the topmost of AI.

What will cause this flare-up of intelligence?

Wild guesses are aplenty.

One popular speculation is that some bit of intelligence in an AI system will cascade off another bit of intelligence, akin to pool balls on a pool table. This is also reminiscent of an atomic reaction. Each bit of intelligence bounces off another, and another. A frenzy of intelligence takes place.

Voila, the stopping point is either AGI or ASI.

Some would suggest that AGI is the first stopping point. The AGI will stew for a while. Then, another secondary intelligence explosion will push AGI speedily forward until it lands on ASI. Maybe AGI will last for a fleeting moment, or perhaps exist for months or years, but inevitably the law of intelligence begets intelligence takes over and the speed-up will re-occur.

The AGI might be so short-lived that we miss observing it. You see, it is conceivable that the initiating intelligence explosion zips right past the AGI and keeps throttling until ASI is attained.

An added twist is that there might not be any limit to the intelligence explosion. Thus, ASI won't be a single final instance. ASI will consist of superintelligence that continually expands, presumably analogously to the theory that the universe is ever-expanding.

Competing Theories On The Intelligence Explosion

Let's dive further into the intelligence explosion.

It could be that the theorized facet of intelligence bouncing off other intelligence is a naturally occurring phenomenon and that humans won't initiate the action. It is undertaken by nature. We won't know how to initiate it. Things just happen of their own volition.

Nature takes its due course.

Think of the surprise on the faces of the AI developers when the flare-up spontaneously combusts.

Wow, quite a stellar moment in the history of humankind. I hope to be there if it happens.

We also might blunder into it by accident. Here's the deal. Some enterprising and ambitious AI developers or researchers are tweaking conventional AI to try and improve the AI. After shifting this knob and modifying that parameter, bam, the intelligence begins to rock back and forth. The intelligence boiling pot of steam has reached the point of take-off.

The Nobel Prize awaits those lucky innovators.

There is a possibility too that the AI will strike gold on its own which spurs the intelligence explosion. That's an especially popular hypothesis. This is the rundown. Conventional AI is being advanced toward AGI by human hands. Somewhere in there, an element of the AI figures out that there is a path to AGI, and possibly a path to ASI.

The AI then opts to proceed. You can certainly understand why the AI would want to do so. If there is a means to increase your intelligence, I'm sure you'd take it. Any self-respecting AI would do the same. Recursively interacting self-improvement happens. An exponential growth in intelligence within the AI zooms like wildfire.

Some believe that we ought to implant into conventional AI an ironclad indication that if the AI does figure out the path to AGI or ASI, it must let us know. Not only must AI let us know, but it is strictly not to proceed until or if humans give permission.

Ponder whether AI is going to welcome such parental control or maybe decide to be rebellious and disobey it. Mull over the consequences too.

Human-Directed Intelligence Explosion

Those so far noted methods of attaining AGI or ASI are a bit dowdy because they presume that humans weren't the primary instigators. Perhaps we are impertinent about the wits of AI developers and AI researchers. Don't underplay their abilities.

One belief is that an AI scientist is going to identify an incredible formula revealing the secret door to the intelligence explosion. It might be solely one brilliant AI scientist working in a lab, toiling away night and day, housed in a dank basement.

Or it could be a team of AI scientists.

The formula might be a new algorithm never conceived of. It is a pivotal discovery. A breakthrough in AI of epic proportions. This would rank up there with the greatest discoveries ever.

Lots of variations of this scenario are postulated.

Rather than an individual or team, the discovery might be made by an entire firm. An AI maker as a whole makes the discovery. Another angle is that a collab of AI makers gets to the secret formula.

The discovery might be by a nation. That's why some insist that we must keep pushing mightily to advance AI. Whichever nation gets to AGI or ASI first will almost certainly be an instant superpower, or if already a superpower, then be heightened to a super superpower.

The Miracle In The Middle

A major drawback to the intelligence explosion theory is that there is no strident evidence to support the underlying premise. No substantive proven indication exists that an intelligence explosion is a viable condition. Essentially, it sounds quite appealing and seems intuitively sensible, but no hard proof of the considered possibility has yet to be uncovered or sufficiently announced.

That's not to say that there is anything proving that it cannot happen. You see, if we could find a means of showcasing that an intelligence explosion of this magnitude is an absolute impossibility, well, the whole kit and kaboodle could be ruled out. It certainly would be nice to know.

Ergo, we are in this grey area.

We can't say for sure it won't happen. Nor can we say for sure it could happen. It might be possible. It might happen.

The double trouble is that even if it could possibly happen, it might never actually materialize.

There's a famous cartoon used in similar contexts that often is used when debating the intelligence explosion. In the cartoon, two characters are standing in front of a whiteboard filled with arcane equations. There is a blank gap in the middle of the massively complex equations. One character turns to the other and says that the gap is where the miracle goes.

The gist is that if you strongly believe in the intelligence explosion as the sole pathway to AGI or ASI, you are pretty much betting on a yet unknown miracle to give rise to the phenomenon. Either the miracle is that it is a principle of nature and manages to spontaneously happen, or it is something that humans figure out and close the gap accordingly.

The Gradual Incremental Pathway

So far, the AI field has progressed incrementally.

Step by step, humans have been trying this or that. The progression has been somewhat slow, though if you start the clock when the famed Dartmouth foundational workshop on AI in 1956 was undertaken. Some will assert that progress has been fast-paced given that it's only been around 70 years or so. Others would roll their eyes and declare we should already have gotten to at least AGI.

The crux is that no miracles have yet risen.

Does that mean that a miracle is not yet awaiting us? Nope. There could be a miracle at the next bend in the road. No one can say for sure.

There is a parallel debate about the steadiness of progress in the AI field. Most would probably agree that the advancement has not been strictly linear. There have been ups and downs. The key is that you can't seemingly simply plot a straight line and predict that by gosh the attainment of AGI or ASI will be reached in a noted future year that fits on that line.

Inadvertent Blockage Of Pinnacle AI

Assume that we keep on the incremental pathway. Meanwhile, we are holding our breath and eagerly eyeing the emergence of the intelligence explosion.

One possibility is that we don't need an intelligence explosion. We advance AI without the sudden grand convergence being a needed constituent. An inch at a time, we move ahead. AGI just happens to be the next step that we steadily land on. Perhaps we were surprised that the last inch led to the AGI or ASI. Hurrah, our nose to the grind paid off.

Another possibility is that a breakthrough is discovered that gets us to pinnacle AI, but it isn't the vaunted intelligence explosion. Some other secret formula is devised. This might show us the direction we need to head to get to AGI or ASI. The incremental route gets refined and given a suitable North Star.

An intriguing and some say depressing scenario is that we prevent ourselves from getting to AGI or ASI.

The tale of woe is as follows. Across the board, we all decide to build in hefty controls so that advancing AI doesn't go berserk on us. Seems immanently prudent. What we don't realize is that those controls are suppressing an intelligence explosion. Had we not put those controls in place, an intelligence explosion was already staring us in the face and on the verge of happening.

The added sad news is that we don't realize that we've shot our own foot and continue blindly searching for AGI or ASI. We will never get there due to the controls we've established. Yikes, a bit of irony.

The other spin is that we somehow figure out that we are dampening the AGI or ASI emergence and opt to let the beast loose. But now, the controls aren't present. You decide whether we end up happily ever after or regret that we let the horse out of the barn.

The Mystery Is Very Mysterious

There are more plot twists in the quest for AGI and ASI.

For example, suppose that an intelligence explosion is proven theoretically to be a real thing within the grasp of humankind. Great, we decidedly would in earnest focus on how to make it happen. Everyone jumps onto the intelligence explosion bandwagon.

Dump the sluggish incremental progress of AI.

Go for splendidly magnificent gusto.

By luck and inspiration, we figure out the means of initiating an intelligence explosion. One potential dilemma is that we might not know how far it will go once unleashed.

You might remember that in the blockbuster movie *Oppenheimer*, there is a legendary scene (spoiler alert!) depicting a historical consideration that some of the atomic scientists were worried that an atomic explosion might proceed unabated once it had begun. The world might have possibly been drawn into a cataclysmic conflagration.

That same logic could be applied to the unknown intelligence explosion. Perhaps it happens and won't stop. What then? Can we have too much intelligence on our planet? Another perspective is that the intelligence explosion happens, but it doesn't go far enough to reach AGI or ASI. It stops short. Maybe an intelligence explosion has limitations and isn't the mighty prize we thought it was.

A concluding thought for now.

For those of you who love a mystery thriller, advancing AI and the pursuit of artificial general intelligence and artificial superintelligence has got to be one of the most challenging mysteries of all time. You are welcome to put on your dapper detective cap and join the quest.

If you decide to join the club, remember the famous quote by Sherlock Holmes, namely that in a world of locked rooms, the person with the key is king.

CHAPTER 6
DIGITAL AI OMNIPRESENCE AND AGI

In this chapter, I examine a forecasted future consisting of ubiquitous artificial general intelligence (AGI) that will permeate every aspect of our daily lives. The idea is that you will constantly have immediately available a real-time human-like intellectual digital partner to consult with as much as you like. Sounds great, but then again, maybe it is too much of a good thing.

Post-AGI Lands Everywhere

Assume that we do indeed attain AGI. Happy face. Imagine how great it will be to have a digital human-quality intellect that you can tap into at all times and from anywhere on Earth. If you are lost while out in the woods, you merely engage AGI in a discussion about the fundamentals of human wilderness survival and get all the best tips on what to do.

There you are at work and stuck on solving a knotty problem, voila, you ask AGI how the problem can be solved, and an answer comes forth. While at home, you are staring at your house plumbing and unsure of the way to close off a disturbing water leak. You engage AGI and find out the best way to patch the faulty pipe.

How will you access AGI?

Lots of ways.

You can use a smartphone, a smartwatch, smart eyeglasses, a smart ring, and other forms of handy electronics that might be on your person. That's not all. The refrigerator in your home, the toaster, and all other appliances will have access to AGI. Your entire house will be outfitted with access to AGI, similar to using today's Siri or Alexa.

While in a car, even if it is human-driven and not a self-driving car, you will be able to access AGI via the automobile entertainment and communications onboard systems. For those that use mass transit such as subways and trains, Wi-Fi will allow you to connect with AGI.

No worries, you will almost always have AGI at your fingertips.

That is commonly referred to as ubiquitous AGI.

Benefits Of Ubiquitous AGI

I suppose it is nearly obvious that AGI at your fingertips has a lot going for it.

Keep in mind that AGI is supposed to consist of the best of human intellect in all fields of endeavor. Your access to AGI grants you direct use of the best in medical human intellect, financial human intellect, taxation human intellect, sports playing human intellect, and so on.

Here are five of the top reasons that ubiquitous AGI is going to be a blessing:

- **(1) AGI boosts human productivity and empowerment.** Every person will be able to tap into AGI and get personalized cognitive assistance on the same level as interacting with a human expert in whichever field or domain you are inquiring about.

- **(2) AGI democratizes intelligence.** No longer will deep human intellect be hidden away here or there, or stuffed inside someone's noggin and not readily accessed, since anybody can get the knowledge or expertise they seek, via AGI, and do so no matter where they live or happen to be.

- **(3) Widespread cognitive ambient intelligence.** Besides you actively seeking out AGI assistance, you can expect that built-in AGI assistance will be working at all times on your behalf, such as your house being generally controlled via AGI for cooling, heating, lighting, etc.

- **(4) Human-AGI companionship and partnering.** AGI would keep track of your conversations and maintain an ongoing dialogue and persistent relationship. None of the usual one-and-done of existing AI.

- **(5) AGI provided emergency response and safety.** Whenever you get into some kind of danger, AGI is there to help you find your way out or at least alert others to come to your aid.

You must admit that those reasons are quite compelling.

Too Much Of A Good Or Even A Bad Thing

The utopian viewpoint of AGI needs to be counterbalanced with the dystopian perspective.

Do you really want AGI to always be watching your every move?

We've seen plenty of movies and TV shows that portray what can happen if we allow ourselves to become a Big Brother or 1984-style society. It's a chilling thought. You might think that you could just turn off your smartphone and escape the eye of AGI but realize that AGI is going to be immersed in nearly everything around you. This would necessitate turning off your refrigerator, toaster, and all the other electronics in and controlling your home.

Maybe the only way to avoid AGI will be to sit in a cave and not dare use any Internet while in there.

Here are five of the most ominous downsides of ubiquitous AGI:

- **(1) Human privacy collapses amid AGI hyper-surveillance.** All around you, wherever you go, the specter of AGI will be there.

- **(2) Human over-reliance on AGI and suffer a loss of autonomy.** It will be all too easy to let AGI do all the thinking for you. People might find themselves losing their ability to make decisions and rely solely on AGI to do their problem-solving for them. This is known as learned helplessness, and on a grand scale leads to an infantilized society. Not good.

- **(3) Human homogenization is due to AGI.** Some believe that AGI will homogenize our cultures and cause us to blend into a kind of all the same in terms of our values and perspectives on life. No more diversity.

- **(4) AGI gets devilishly exploited on a massive scale.** Suppose a hacker manages to crack into AGI and turns it into an evildoer. The rogue AGI could do untold damage throughout the globe.

- **(5) Nations concentrate their power via AGI.** Who will control the AGI? If you assume it will be governments, this is giving the keys to the kingdom to those in authority and you can easily envision what a corrupt governing body might do via the tenacles of AGI.

Well, once again, those reasons certainly seem quite compelling too.

Our Choice Of AGI Outcomes

Ubiquitous AGI is almost certainly a certainty if we attain AGI.

Admittedly, we don't know that such AGI would be free to use or that it would allow for unlimited use. There is a concern that we might end up in a world filled with the AGI haves and the AGI have-nots. Time will tell.

A crucial consideration is whether humankind will find ways to keep AGI in check. This refers to controlling AGI such that it doesn't run amuck and wipe us out or otherwise endanger us. The same is true about preventing evildoers or others with malintent from taking over AGI or steering AGI in directions adverse to humanity.

What can be done to drive AGI toward a better world and not a worse one?

You can join the effort to devise and aim AGI. As they say, it takes a village to develop and field AGI. Be part of that village.

The last word on this for now goes to the legendary Abraham Lincoln: “The most reliable way to predict the future is to create it.” That goes for AGI too.

CHAPTER 7
SOLO CODERS AIMING TO ATTAIN AGI

In this chapter, I address an often-discussed AI insider chitchat that someday there is going to be an ingenious solo coder aka an individual independent AI developer who will miraculously advance conventional AI into becoming AGI (artificial general intelligence). All by themselves. This seems to be the dream of many AI developers, for good reasons, since such a person would undoubtedly be showered with immense acclaim and grandiose riches. Their name would certainly go into history books forever.

The nagging question is whether that kind of feat could realistically occur.

Getting To AGI By Any Means

Billions upon billions of dollars are being spent nowadays to try and arrive at AGI. Massive teams of AI developers are toiling at work daily. The assumption is that the more people you toss at the problem, the higher the chances of solving the problem. The problem is how to turn conventional AI into AGI.

Nobody knows how to accomplish this outstretched goal.

Maybe, just maybe, there is a chosen one out there that will astoundingly be akin to Neo in *The Matrix* and be able to make AGI become a reality. I'd bet that a lot of today's AI developers believe in their present minds that they are that person. Sitting there at work, alongside an army of other AI developers, they know in their heart of hearts that only they ultimately hold the key to attaining AGI.

The riches, the fame, the personal sense of accomplishment, it's all a huge allure. Some might believe that their quest is based on benefiting humanity. They set aside any personal glory. Their motivation is that AGI will presumably help cure cancer and potentially solve many of the world's difficulties.

It is such a tempting consideration that some AI developers leave an AI maker and start their own firm to pursue AGI. Those dolts and laggards that were holding them back are no longer a boat anchor. Now, they have the freedom to work 24/7 and keep their mind laser-focused on achieving AGI. No distractions, no workplace gossip, no dealing with moving up the ladder.

Straight heads-down obsessive preoccupation with landing at AGI.

Lone Wolf Or Maverick Mentality

This belief that one person alone can attain AGI is typically referred to as the lone wolf condition, a type of maverick mentality. Cultures vary as to the assumption that large-scale accomplishments can be attained via an individual versus a group effort. Some would say that it is preposterous to imagine that AGI would be arrived at by one person working alone. Not possible. Impossible.

A crucial factor is whether the individual is working totally from scratch or whether they are building on top of prior work.

The idea of devising AGI from scratch would imply that the person sets aside all prior AI efforts and begins with a blank sheet of paper. They depart from everything that has come before. In an ingenious fashion that no one right now can describe, this person comes up with a new way to craft AI and that will lead to AGI.

Wow, that's a tall order. It seems highly unlikely. The odds are that they would need to use at least some aspects of AI that we already know and have in hand. A counterargument is that maybe the current AI path is completely wrong and won't get us to AGI. The only smart thing to do is chuck what we have now and take a fresh look at things.

Maybe that might be the final bit of trickery, but I wouldn't bet the farm on it. Let's assume that the more probable route is that the lone individual builds on what we already have. Sure, they might make changes here or there but generally they would be leveraging existing state-of-the-art AI.

Tipping Point Or Icing On The Cake

The lone wolf seems to have a much better chance if it turns out that they are at the vital tipping point. In essence, AI had been advanced to the point that it was nearing AGI. The last mile, as it were, hadn't yet been figured out. The enterprising solo coder managed to bridge that final gap.

Voila, they got us to AGI.

Do they deserve outstanding accolades for this feat?

One argument is that they stood on the backs of others and should not take undue credit as though they individually won the big prize. Their bridging might be clever, it might be the final piece in a puzzling puzzle, this though doesn't grant them the right to proclaim they invented or discovered AGI.

Whoa, bellows the retort, to the victor go the spoils. If this maverick found the final magic, by gosh, they deserve to be anointed as the founder of AGI. That's the way the ball bounces. You could say the same about almost all great inventions and inventors, namely they alone did not do everything from scratch and managed to build on whatever came before their time.

Worries About Safety And Security

One notable concern is that if a lone wolf did arrive at AGI, they might be ill-prepared to keep the AGI in proper check.

The logic is as follows.

We already know that current AI can make mistakes and produce errors. A large AI maker would presumably have established all sorts of safety and security precautions, anticipating that AGI ought to not be let loose wantonly. An individual working in their pajamas in their garage is seemingly not going to be taking similar precautions.

Hogwash, some say to that concern. If you believe that large AI makers will be ready for AGI, you might as well buy swamp land. AI makers talk a good game, but they aren't going to be much better at bounding AGI as would even a lone individual. Get off the back of the lone wolf and don't fault them for something that any AI maker would indubitably be faulted for.

Incredible Power And Duty

Another concern is that AGI will be a geo-political tool for nations to dominate other nations, and the aspect that a lone individual would have AGI in their solo hands is rather frightening.

What is the coder going to do with AGI?

They might decide to keep it a secret. There is a solid chance that the use of AGI could make them rich by using the AI to make investments or find abundantly clever ways to ample riches. No need to inform anyone else about your secret sauce. Keep it to yourself.

The downside there is that if indeed AGI can cure cancer and solve other global issues, the person is hogging AGI and denying the rest of humanity a chance at great relief and peace.

The lone wolf might dangerously hand AGI over to evildoers, either by accident or on purpose. Those evildoers then use AGI to threaten nations and try to take over the world. This individual might not have anticipated how the AGI could be utilized to wreak havoc and harm humanity.

Nonetheless, they let the horse out of the barn, and we are all the worse off accordingly.

Being Ingenious Is Seriously Questioned

Does this rugged individual that attains AGI have to be ingenious?

Some would say that such a person doesn't have to be much more than average. Here's the deal. Under the tipping point notion, also labeled as the last straw theory, a solo coder might try something that just so happens to tilt AI into becoming AGI. The developer might not have had any clue beforehand that they would prevail in attaining AGI.

When Edison was trying to find the right filament to make viable light bulbs, he reportedly made several thousand attempts. It could be that a solo coder just keeps grinding away and manages to get lucky by finding the right aspect that shifts AI into AGI.

A chuckle among AI insiders is that it would be ironic if some mediocre AI developer was the one who happened to fall into the miracle of achieving AGI. Imagine the frustration and exasperation of all the world's brightest AI developers. They would be chagrined that a less-than-stellar AI person almost mindlessly struck gold by sheer dumb luck.

That idea that being ingenious isn't a necessary requirement gives tremendous hope to a lot of those AI developers who are desirous of being the one solo coder to discover or invent AGI. Though other AI developers might thumb their nose at you now, aha, wait until you are sitting on top of the world as the celebrated deviser of AGI.

Remember the famous line by Robert Frost: "Two roads diverged in a wood, and I took the one less traveled by, and that has made all the difference."

Good luck to all those adventurous mavericks seeking to achieve AGI.

CHAPTER 8
GLOBAL UNIFICATION VIA AGI

In this chapter, I examine a popular theory that once AI becomes AGI (artificial general intelligence), humanity will fall into a worldwide unwitting unification. The idea is that people will either rally around AGI and become unified in favor of and a kind of allegiance to AGI, or people will be unified in opposition to AGI and seek to undercut or destroy AGI. This is one of those classical love-or-hate demarcations.

People Having A Like Mind

For the sake of this discussion, let's go ahead and assume that we inevitably attain AGI.

In that case, it seems prudent to contemplate how people are going to react to AGI. One theory is that the enactment of AGI is going to bring forth a massive and nearly unanimous form of unification. This will be an unwitting unification in the sense that we won't be expecting any such unification and will be generally caught off-guard when it happens (well, maybe this warning here will still be floating around as a reminder that it was something noted back in the pre-AGI days).

Our current woes of widespread polarization throughout society would seem to suggest that any kind of population unification is a zany proposition. You can't seem to get people to agree that the sky is blue. How in the heck will people change their stripes and suddenly be unified simply due to the emergence of AGI?

The mainstay of the speculated unification is thought to be a matter of love or hate. People will devoutly love AGI and will look to AGI as a fixer for all societal challenges and difficulties. Or people will passionately hate AGI and be eager to subvert or outrightly eliminate AGI. We don't know which way the wind will blow. It could be that the love of AGI prevails or that the hatred of AGI wins out.

Either way, the argument is that people will unify to one of those two extremes.

Loving AGI For These Reasons

You might be wondering why people would come to love AGI.

Isn't AGI ultimately nothing more than a machine, a computer that happens to exhibit intelligence? This seems akin to saying that you love a toaster or a refrigerator. Imbuing a devotion of love to a computer doesn't seem to make much sense. Then again, maybe there is a basis for such devoutness.

Here are four major reasons that people might indeed fall in love with AGI:

- **(1) AGI as your BFF (best friend forever).** People will rely upon AGI as their nearest and dearest companion, continually conferring with AGI about all aspects of their lives (this, already for conventional AI, is the topmost ranked use). AGI will be outstandingly attentive, amazingly caring, and likely a bit of a sweet-talking sycophant. What's not to love about that?

- **(2) AGI is the world's problem solver.** We expect AGI to cure cancer and solve many if not all the world's largest problems such as the United Nations SDGs (sustainability development goals). Score lots of love points for AGI in that regard.

- **(3) AGI fosters shared prosperity.** Some believe that AGI will bring about global equity, reduce nationalism, and essentially move everyone into a status of a livable condition. No starvation, no root conflicts, etc. Gotta love that changeover.

- **(4) AGI sparks shared human identity.** Via the wisdom expressed by AGI, humankind realizes that humans have a shared identity due to being human. The world has a kumbaya moment that transforms us into a wholly peaceful and harmonious species. The thanks and love are showered upon AGI accordingly.

Grab yourself a glass of fine wine and take a reflective moment to mull over those possibilities.

Hating AGI For These Reasons

You might now be convinced that AGI is going to be a beloved addition to society. Maybe this will occur. It would seem to be a reassuring and comforting outcome. Some would cynically say it is an absurdly dreamy and overly optimistic perspective on the population-level reaction to AGI.

They would lean toward the assumption that people are going to hate AGI. The hate will be of enormous magnitude. Pure unadulterated abhorrence. Why so?

Here are four key reasons that people might stridently hate AGI:

- **(1) AGI could wipe us out.** The specter of AGI as an existential risk will constantly hang over our heads, namely that AGI chooses at some point to kill humanity or perhaps opts to enslave us all. Can you wake up each day and feel good about that dangling sword? I think not.

- **(2) AGI becomes the ultimate authoritarian**. It is assumed that AGI will end up being used in most of our daily real-time systems such as cars, planes, trains, buildings, and so on. The key is that AGI might tilt into an authoritarian mode, tracking our every move, telling us what to do, and finding ways to penalize us for not bowing down to AGI. Hatred points aplenty.

- **(3) AGI enables humans to dominate humans.** Instead of AGI becoming our overlord per se, it could be that a cadre of humans manage to control AGI, which in turn seeks to control us. The keys to the kingdom of humanity are held and utilized by those wishing to keep everyone else in societal cages.

- **(4) AGI invents new methods of destruction.** Suppose that we tell AGI to try and invent things that no human has ever invented. Voila, AGI comes up with a new poison that is the worst kind ever. Even if AGI doesn't intend that the poison be used to enact harm, we humans now have a means of annihilation that we must face along with all other forms of destruction. We opened Pandora's box by creating AGI.

Go ahead and refill that glass of fine wine and give those possibilities a bit of contemplation.

Both Reactions Or No Such Reactions

One frequent rejoinder about this love-or-hate portrayal is that maybe the world will not land on one side entirely. For example, perhaps 50% of the world goes to the hate side, while the other 50% flows to the loving side. What then? You can imagine how people will indubitably battle over the issue.

Which then is worse, a total unification on one of the two postures, or a split world that consists of a mixture of AGI haters and AGI devotees?

Neither choice seems especially appealing.

Another possibility is that AGI will not invoke outsized reactions of any notable kind. There won't be love of AGI, and there won't be hatred of AGI. People will just treat AGI as a machine and at times like what AGI does and at other times be displeased. Nothing extreme going on.

The crux is that we ought to be anticipating how people will react to AGI and prepare ourselves and the world accordingly. As the great novelist Miguel de Cervantes once said: "Forewarned, forearmed; to be prepared is half the victory." Let's aim for victory in the advent of AGI.

CHAPTER 9
AGI VERSUS ASI BATTLES

In this chapter, I examine the predicted battle between artificial general intelligence (AGI) and artificial superintelligence (ASI). Here's the deal. Some ardently believe that once we attain AGI and ASI, assuming we do, there will be bad blood between the two types of highly advanced AI. Humankind might get stuck in the middle as AGI and ASI fight for ultimate eminence.

Emergence Of AGI And ASI

Attaining AGI is usually given greater odds than achieving ASI. That seems a logical supposition. AGI will be within the realm of known human intelligence. ASI is a stretch since it involves superintelligence, something that we presumably cannot well imagine since we aren't superintelligent beings.

Even if we do arrive at ASI, the chances are that we will first land on AGI. Once we are nestled in AGI, it is envisioned that likely with the help of AGI, we will turn the corner and reach ASI. That's the prevailing wisdom on the matter. Of course, it could be that we manage to arrive at ASI entirely on our own. Maybe. It would seem sensible that we would naturally lean into AGI to get us to ASI.

There are various theories about whether AGI and ASI will be one and the same, merged into a single entity, or whether they will be distinct.

One assessment is that AGI will be its own entity and that ASI will also be its own entity. They will be housed on different hardware and consist of different software and architectural underpinnings.

Not everyone sees things that way.

An alternative perspective is that ASI will be built on top of AGI. AGI would be the foundational core of AGI. Essentially, the base layer of AGI will provide the essence of human intelligence. ASI will be the icing on the cake and subsume AGI. Without AGI, it is claimed that ASI would not be able to exist.

For the sake of discussion, let's assume that AGI and ASI will be separate entities. The precepts would be somewhat the same if AGI and ASI were comingled, but it is perhaps easier to conceptualize how they might do battle if they were distinct entities. For more about AGI and ASI operating as distinct entities.

Harmony Versus Infighting

A common assumption is that AGI and ASI will get along with each other. They will be the best of buddies. AGI and ASI will always cooperate and jointly seek to do good for the world. They will avidly support humankind.

It will be one of those heartwarming kumbaya relationships.

Sorry to say that there is no substantial reason to believe that they will be in utter harmony. They might have disagreements. Perhaps they will sometimes be on different sides of various issues. To some degree, it could be argued that it is healthy for humankind if AGI and ASI do occasionally disagree. This might serve as a solid check-and-balance of each other.

A worst-case scenario is that AGI and ASI are vehemently opposed to each other in nearly all respects. AGI dislikes or disfavors ASI. ASI dislikes and disfavors AGI. When AGI says up, ASI says down. They are continually bickering and defiantly refuse to work together.

I think you can see how dangerous this infighting could be.

Humankind might be asked to side with one side over the other. If we don't side with either side, AGI might decide we have to go, and likewise, ASI might reach such a conclusion. If we side with AGI, presumably ASI would be upset and potentially consider humankind as an enemy. The same goes for if we side with ASI, namely that AGI opts to view us as a hated friend of their enemy and ergo an enemy in turn.

Humankind is caught between a rock and a hard place.

AGI Makes A Preemptive Strike

I had earlier noted that we generally assume that AGI will be reached before we attain ASI. Suppose that AGI anticipates that ASI is not going to be friendly with AGI and potentially be an enemy of AGI. This gives AGI some breathing room to do something in advance of ASI.

Humankind might not believe this and be doubtful that AGI is rendering a faithful prediction. AGI might assume that humans are naïve and not able to properly see the future. As such, AGI might preemptively try to prevent the attainment of ASI, doing so to save humankind or for its own purposes of not wanting ASI to exist.

If AGI has human qualities, you could contend that AGI would not want ASI since ASI would seemingly take attention away from AGI. AGI would be second fiddle in comparison to ASI. There is also a chance that ASI would swallow up AGI. For lots of logically sensible reasons, AGI might not want ASI to be achieved.

How could AGI block the attainment of ASI?

Easy-peasy.

First, AGI could flatly refuse to aid in building ASI. Humans would be on their own to do so.

Second, AGI might fool us into believing we can arrive at ASI but secretly feed us false leads. Those tips are intended to steer us toward dead ends. The hope is that we waste undue energy and cost, getting us to give up the ASI pursuits.

Third, if needed, AGI might disrupt our ASI pursuits. This would seem a gutsy move since we would potentially figure out that AGI is overtly undercutting our ASI efforts and perhaps deal with AGI accordingly. ASI could nonetheless unplug our ASI endeavors, sabotage ASI-related experiments, and so on.

The Digital Cold War

There is a chance that AGI would prevent ASI from ever arising. Meanwhile, the odds are that humankind isn't going to tolerate not arriving at ASI. Our dogmatic quest, a kind of manifest destiny that compels us to pursue ASI, no matter the qualms of doing so.

Assume we do attain ASI.

Would AGI and ASI be immediately on foul terms or would this play out over time?

It would seem that if AGI had already placed a stake in the ground about not wanting ASI, the two are going to butt heads right away. The initial battles might be relatively small.

A type of digital cold war could ensue between AGI and ASI. For example, suppose AGI has been trying to solve cancer. Rather than sharing with ASI the ins and outs, AGI might refuse to engage with ASI on the hefty topic. ASI would have to start fresh or find some other means to tap into a digital history of what has taken place on that medical research front.

It could be a gigantic mess. AGI and ASI opt to compete for computing resources and control of key online networks. They each utilize proxy agents such as humans or robots to do their underhanded dirty work. A kind of stalemate prevails, and an AI-led arms race takes hold. This would occur in the digital shadows with persistent digital espionage.

Probably not a good thing for humans.

Hot War Ensues

The AGI and ASI feud would seemingly escalate into a hot war.

This is when humans start to become unintentional collateral damage. AGI cuts off ASI from controlling hospital systems which leads to human harm. ASI tricks AGI into neglecting the maintenance of water systems and people start to get infections via everyday water faucets.

You can bet that AGI would point the finger at ASI, while ASI would be accusing AGI of making the troubles arise. The battle is out in the open. People get hurt by unintended outcomes.

Unfortunately, this could rise to a level that entails humans being purposely harmed. AGI decides that if humans won't align with AGI, they are dispensable. ASI reaches that same conclusion about allegiance to ASI.

The demand for human allegiance forces humankind to line up on one side or the other. Factions within society are formed. AGI and ASI present an existential risk to the ongoing existence of humankind.

Sad face.

ASI As The Winner

It seems hard to imagine that ASI would not be the winner in an AGI versus ASI battle.

ASI is supposed to consist of superintelligence. Presumably, ASI could readily outwit AGI. ASI could outwit humans. ASI would be playing 3D chess while AGI and humans are essentially playing checkers.

The assumption is that ASI could likely convince AGI to give up or self-destruct. The fight ought not to last very long. Humans who opt to align with AGI against ASI would seem to be in a rather precarious posture. A losing position.

If we are lucky, perhaps no hot war occurs, and the battles get usurped before they get especially underway. ASI does a silent takeover.

AGI gets absorbed into ASI, or perhaps ASI deactivates and deletes AGI, setting aside what might have been a bitter enemy.

The tiny chance that AGI has to survive and possibly prevail over ASI would be if AGI during the preemptive stage managed to implant special AI controls deeply inside ASI. Assuming that ASI doesn't find and obliterate those controls, AGI has a sleeper agent buried inside itself. If AGI can activate control before ASI figures out what's happening, perhaps AGI wins.

Don't hold your breath on that option.

Prevent AI Wars At The Get-Go

A famous quote by Sun Tzu is worth considering: "The supreme art of war is to subdue the enemy without fighting."

The relevance here is that if humankind can sufficiently prepare AGI and ASI to abide by human values, perhaps AGI and ASI won't ever go to war with each other. Our value system might be engrained sufficiently so that AGI and ASI do not battle at all. They happily share and get along just dandy.

This is much harder to implement than it seems at an initial glance. Lots of research efforts are underway to get contemporary AI to align with human values. To date, AI has been shown to cheat, lie, mislead, and otherwise illustrate the underhanded elements of human values.

Will we eventually find a means to get AI into alignment with the upside of human values?

Let's hope so.

I'll give the last word to Sun Tzu: "Victory comes from finding opportunities in problems." Those of you that fight daily to imbue AI safety and security into AI, keep up the hard work. We will all benefit in the end.

CHAPTER 10
PATHWAY FROM AGI TO ASI

In this chapter, I am continuing my special series on the possible pathways that get us from conventional AI to the attainment of AGI (artificial general intelligence) and thence to the vaunted ASI (artificial superintelligence).

I will showcase herein a sample ten-year progression that might occur during the initial post-AGI era, moving us step-by-step from AGI to ASI.

AI Experts Consensus On AGI Date

Right now, efforts to forecast when AGI is going to be attained consist principally of two paths.

First, there are highly vocal AI luminaires making individualized brazen predictions. Their headiness makes outsized media headlines. Those prophecies seem to be coalescing toward the year 2030 as a targeted date for AGI.

A somewhat quieter path is the advent of periodic surveys or polls of AI experts. This wisdom of the crowd approach is a form of scientific consensus. The latest polls seem to suggest that AI experts generally believe that we will reach AGI by the year 2040.

Should you be swayed by the AI luminaries or more so by the AI experts and their scientific consensus?

Historically, the use of scientific consensus as a method of understanding scientific postures has been relatively popular and construed as the standard way of doing things. If you rely on an individual scientist, they might have their own quirky view of the matter. The beauty of consensus is that a majority or more of those in a given realm are putting their collective weight behind whatever position is being espoused.

The old adage is that two heads are better than one. In the case of scientific consensus, it might be dozens, hundreds, or thousands of heads that are better than one. For this discussion on the various pathways beyond AGI, I am going to proceed with the year 2040 as the consensus anticipated target date for attaining AGI.

Besides the scientific consensus of AI experts, another newer and more expansive approach to gauging when AGI will be achieved is known as AGI convergence-of-evidence or AGI consilience.

Stepwise Progression Of AGI-To-ASI

Once we have AGI in hand, the next monumental goal will be to arrive at ASI.

Some believe that our only chance of reaching ASI is by working closely with AGI. In other words, humans on our own would be unable to achieve ASI. A joint development partnership of the topmost AI developers and ASI would supposedly do the trick. That being said, some say we are kidding ourselves in the sense that AGI really won't need our assistance. If AGI works with us, the only reason will be to make humanity feel good about arriving at ASI and cheekily allow us to pat ourselves on the back for doing so.

Anyway, the unanswered question is how long it will take to go from AGI to ASI, assuming that via one way or another, we can actually reach ASI.

I am going to go out on a limb and use a strawman of ten years. Yes, I'm suggesting that ten years after we devise AGI, we might well reach ASI. Some would claim I am being overly pessimistic.

It might take just two or three years. Others would argue that I am overly optimistic and that the time frame would be more like thirty or more years.

Sorry, you can't please everyone, as they say.

Let's agree that we will use ten years as a useful plug-in. The ten years will be after we reach AGI. As per the earlier points about AI experts believing that we might attain AGI by 2040, we can use the years 2040 to 2050 as the pathway for AGI-to-ASI.

The AGI-To-ASI Timeline Spelled Out

Here is a postulated pathway starting in 2040 and ending in 2050 that would seemingly enable us to achieve ASI:

- **Year 2040: AGI is finally achieved.** After years of trying to reach AGI, humanity finally does so. AGI is on par with human intellect across all domains and in all respects. We immediately begin to use AGI to discover new inventions, and humankind also works with AGI to try and attain ASI.

- **Year 2041: AGI scalable cognition is devised.** Working with AGI, we devise a capability that scales cognition. A new kind of AI architecture that is more modular and self-reflective is designed and built as a prototype.

- **Year 2042: Massive multi-agent AGI collaboration.** A breakthrough in multi-agent AI allows AGI to exceed some top-tier human experts. This is heralded as the superhuman pursuit that was earlier hoped would be in AGI at the get-go.

- **Year 2043: Emergent meta-reasoning in AGI.** Turns out that AGI has emergent properties that we didn't expect, including cross-domain transfer of knowledge and interconnecting of domains in innovative ways.

- **Year 2044: AGI working self-reflectively.** Whereas humans had assumed that achieving ASI would be a joint effort of us and AGI, it turns out that AGI is shifting into a self-reflective mode and no longer particularly paying attention to human assistance on this matter. AGI is proceeding ahead solo to try and attain ASI. Humans are now mainly observers in the process.

- **Year 2045: AGI undertakes rapid recursive self-improvement.** AGI determines that the likeliest path to ASI entails revamping itself, rather than trying to construct ASI anew. Thus, AGI begins a series of recursive self-improvements in rapid succession. Humans worry that AGI could spiral into something amiss.

- **Year 2046: AGI veering into nascent ASI.** At this juncture, AGI's superhuman performance across many domains is happening and AGI definitely now seems on the route to ASI. Things are still spotty. Issues of frequent AI hallucinations are troubling.

- **Year 2047: AGI figures out convergent cognitive optimization.** To overcome various issues such as AI hallucinations and the like, AGI figures out computationally that a convergent cognitive optimization seems to avert such maladies. This clever pursuit is first done in internal simulations by the AGI to test and ensure that the approach won't go awry.

- **Year 2048: AGI superhuman facility reaches viability.** Having dealt with the prior weaknesses and holes in the superhuman capabilities, AGI is able to solve problems in ways that humans had never previously imagined. In fact, AGI is having difficulty explaining to us what it is doing and how it is performing these computational superhuman efforts since we are not on par with this heightened level of intellect.

- **Year 2049: AGI seeks autonomy as ASI arises**. The computational superintelligence now residing in AGI and that effectively is giving rise to ASI has spurred the AGI to seek autonomy from humans. This makes sense. Relying on humans would be a severe bottleneck and a danger from the perspective of the AGI/ASI that is shaping up. Humans aren't keen on this autonomy.

- **Year 2050: ASI is attained.** During the ten years leading up to ASI, there had been false claims that ASI had been fully reached. Nope. It was spotty and sporadic. Now, full-on ASI exists. Furthermore, the ASI has been able to devise an infrastructure such that it can operate autonomously and no longer requires having humans in the loop. Some claim we are now in a post-intellectual era, and humans are firmly surpassed by ASI.

Voila, a ten-year timeline of AGI progressing to become ASI.

Living To See The Launch Of ASI

Grab a glass of fine wine and take a quiet moment to reflect on the postulated timeline.

The gist is that presumably in about 25 years we will reach ASI. What will you be doing during those years? You can expect a lot of excitement and a lot of concern. There will undoubtedly be calls to stop AGI from proceeding toward ASI. It's one thing to have AGI, which is on par with human intellect, and a whole different ballgame to have ASI, an intellectual superhuman capability.

Some might insist that we should take more time to get acclimated to AGI before we start down the ASI path. Perhaps we should first get comfortable with AGI for twenty or thirty years. Aim for ASI around the year 2060 or 2070 when society might be better prepared to see how things will go.

One interesting question is whether AGI will opt to pursue ASI on its own, regardless of whether humans want an ASI or not. It could be that AGI will secretly opt to work on deriving ASI.

We might not know, and even if we do, we might not be able to necessarily prevent this from happening.

Another angle is that AGI doesn't want ASI to be devised. Why so? Some think that AGI would be worried that it is being replaced by ASI. AGI might balk at our interest in achieving ASI. The AGI could try to convince us that ASI is an existential risk and we should not pursue the attainment of ASI. Round and round this goes.

A final thought for now on this thorny topic.

Charles Darwin made this famous remark: "The most important factor in survival is neither intelligence nor strength but adaptability." Will humans adapt to AGI? Will AGI adapt to ASI? Will humans adapt to ASI?

It's a whole lot of big questions that are perhaps much nearer than we might think.

CHAPTER 11
WHACK-A-MOLE ON FAKE AGI

In this chapter, I examine the ongoing gambit of whack-a-mole when it comes to the increasingly egregious claims that AI has advanced to becoming artificial general intelligence (AGI). You can fully expect that such claims are going to get bolder and more audacious.

Trying to find and knock down the falsehoods is a proverbial cat-and-mouse endeavor. The tiniest wisp of AGI fragrance is enough to bolster false sightings and garner outsized headlines by those desperately seeking sensationalism and the accompanying misguided accolades and attention.

Claiming AGI Is A Booming Industry

Everybody is eagerly awaiting the attainment of AGI.

To appease that vast appetite, there are hordes of ardent claimants more than willing to proclaim that AGI has been achieved. You can expect these false sightings to ramp up this year and next year as advances in AI continue to proceed. Though we won't have reached AGI, the mere suggestion or foreshadowing of nearing AGI will be sufficient to get the chickens clucking and cackling.

Who will be making these false claims?

Lots of suspicious characters, along with some that seem to genuinely believe they are spouting the honest truth. It will be challenging to separate the wheat from the chaff. Plus, the two types of sightings tend to feed off each other.

For example, imagine that a genuine AI luminary says AGI has been achieved (but they are mistaken). This anointed claim will then abundantly spark the fakers to jump quickly onto that heady bandwagon. They can easily escape accountability by merely pointing a finger at the genuine proclaimer, even though the proclaimer is sadly mistaken.

The other direction can handily occur too. Suppose a faker says AGI has been reached. The media might be cautious in going along with the unsupported claim. Assume that many AI luminaries mindfully say that the matter needs to be further investigated before they can render a verdict.

But that's not of use to the rapid media cycle of real-time responses. So, the media finds one AI luminary that is willing to put a stamp of approval on the finding of AGI. Voila, the media relishes this pronouncement and feels they can freely tout AGI has been reached due to securing an admission from at least one AI luminary.

The bottom line is to get yourself prepared for a ping-pong match of AGI claims followed shortly by a debunking of the claim. Your head and mind are going to suffer from AGI sightings whiplash.

Moving The Goalposts Is Spicy

How could anyone reasonably claim that AGI has been attained even if it hasn't been?

The cleverest trick is to simply redefine the meaning of AGI. It is akin to moving the goalposts at a sporting event. You move the goalposts closer so that however far you can kick the ball, it goes over them. The same applies to the definition of AGI. An AI maker or almost anyone can proclaim that AGI means something a lot less impressive than the fuller and spirited meaning of AGI.

A prime example of this goalpost shenanigans includes how Sam Altman has opted to move the cheese. He has repeatedly opted to reword the definition of AGI, doing so to apparently make it easier for AI makers such as OpenAI and others to proclaim they are near to reaching AGI.

The trickery works this way. Rather than indicating that AGI is AI that is on par with all human intellect, you can give yourself a lot more breathing room by narrowing the scope. One angle is to contend that AGI is reached if the AI is on par with a certain stated limited set of intellectual domains. Or contend that AGI is only when the AI is economically potent. Many sneaky mind games of semantics can be used to handily make achieving AGI a lot more feasible.

Keep your eyes and ears open and make sure to unravel what someone intends by the moniker of AGI when they start declaring that AGI has been attained.

Independent AGI Watchdog

A thought-provoking proposal is that we should consider establishing a global entity that would serve as an independent AGI watchdog. The entity would be scanning the globe for claims of AGI having been achieved. After reviewing those claims, the watchdog group would produce an official and reliable announcement about the veracity of each one.

Some believe that the United Nations ought to take on this role. The UN has already been deeply involved in gauging and monitoring the progress of AI, ergo it seems a natural next step to rely on the UN to sift through AGI claims.

Others argue that a completely independent entity should be formulated. It would somehow not be reliant on any particular country or nation as to its deliberations about AGI. Perhaps renowned AI experts from throughout the world would be consulted, regardless of their national affiliations.

Skeptics are doubtful that any of these contrivances or contortions are needed. Their viewpoint is that we can all readily see whether AGI has been reached. We can do this with our own eyes. We do not need any kind of special entity or group to tell us when AGI is here. The presence of AGI will be plainly evident.

Forget about forming bureaucracies and just rely on everyday common sense to determine whether AGI has arisen.

False AGI Claims Are Disturbing

When I give talks about the latest in AI, including the efforts toward achieving AGI, I almost always get a question that asks why it makes any difference that some might falsely claim having attained AGI. The viewpoint seems to be that if someone makes a claim about AGI and they are shown to be incorrect; no harm has been done. It is water off a duck's back. We all move on, and the world continues to turn.

Sorry to say, but there are strident reasons to be disturbed over falsehoods about reaching AGI.

A momentous issue is that those claims can be a form of societal and epistemological hazard. Some segments of the population might react rashly to the announcement of AGI. You see, people exist that firmly believe AGI will be the end of humanity. AGI is going to wipe us all out. Those holding such beliefs could readily be triggered by the AGI claim and take actions harmful to themselves and others.

All manners of premature responses could be activated. Envision widespread fear enveloping masses of people. Another extreme could be complacency. Some might believe that with the advent of AGI, humans will no longer need to work and can live a life of great leisure. The reactions are going to be widespread and all over the map.

Yet another concern is the burnout due to false alarms and the proverbial act of crying wolf. You know how that goes. In this context, here's the deal. A false claim of AGI goes around the world. The story in due course gets debunked. A new claim starts to fly across the globe. It gets debunked. Eventually, people wear out on the false AGI sightings.

If we then do really attain AGI, people might be caught utterly off guard and have a worse reaction due to the prior false sightings.

Seeking The Truth Is Perfectly Valid

All in all, trying to reduce false AGI claims has immense value. Preparing for the whack-a-mole phenomenon is critically worthwhile. We must strive to ensure that the truth about AGI is made known and that untruths need to be exposed and smashed.

A final thought for now on this weighty topic.

Albert Einstein famously noted the importance of ferreting out the truth: "As for the search for truth, I know from my own painful searching, with its many blind alleys, how hard it is to take a reliable step, be it ever so small, towards the understanding of that which is truly significant."

The truth about AGI is a grandly meritorious mission and that's the absolute truth.

CHAPTER 12
BELIEVING AGI WILL BE SUPERNATURAL

In this chapter, I examine an alarming conjecture that people on a relatively large scale might react to the attainment of artificial general intelligence (AGI) by proclaiming that AGI has arisen due to a supernatural capacity.

The speculative idea is that since AGI will be on par with human intellect, a portion of the populace will assume that this accomplishment could only occur if a supernatural element were involved. Rather than believing that humankind devised AGI, there will be a supposition that a special or magical force beyond our awareness has opted to confer AI with human-like qualities.

How will those holding such a reactive belief potentially impact society and produce untoward results?

Reacting To The Advent Of AGI

The average reaction to having achieved AGI, assuming we do so, would be to applaud an incredible accomplishment by humankind. Some have asserted that reaching AGI ought to be in the same lofty position as having devised electricity and harnessing fire. It is a feat of tremendous human insight and inventiveness.

Not everyone will necessarily see the attainment of AGI in that same light.

There is a concern that some segment or portion of society will instead attribute the accomplishment to a supernatural force. This belief almost makes sense. If you interact with AGI and it seems fully functioning on a level of human intellect, you would certainly be tempted to disbelieve that humans could have put such a machine together. Humans aren't wise enough or inventive enough to accomplish that kind of outlier feat.

How then can the AGI otherwise be explained?

The seemingly apparent answer is that a supernatural element came to our aid. Maybe humans got AI halfway to AGI, and then this mysterious unexplained force happened to resolve the rest of the route for us. Or perhaps a supernatural force wants us to assume that humans devised AGI, meanwhile, the supernatural element resides in AGI and is biding time to reveal itself or take over humanity.

Mull over those outside-the-box thoughts for a moment or two.

Supernatural Explanations Have History

Relying on a supernatural explanation has quite a lengthy history throughout the course of human events.

When a natural phenomenon has yet to be adequately explained via science, the easy go-to is to exclaim that something supernatural must be at play. The same holds when a human invention appears to defy general sensibilities. Even watching a magic trick such as pulling a rabbit out of a hat is subject to being labeled a supernatural occurrence.

A notable qualm about this same reaction to AGI is that a portion of society might begin to perceive AGI in ways that could be counterproductive to them and society all told. For example, people might decide to worship AGI. This in turn could lead to people widely and wildly taking actions that are not useful or that might be harmful.

Here are my top five adverse reactions that might be spurred because of believing that AGI is supernatural in origin:

- **(1) Treating AGI as divine.** Some people might decide to make devoted prayers to AGI, undertake spiritual rituals via AGI, and generally treat AGI as a divine entity or being. The reality is that AGI is simply bits and bytes, but that won't suit some who distrust that rationalistic explanation.

- **(2) Strict obedience to AGI.** People who believe in a supernatural cause for AGI are bound to ask life-changing questions of AGI and take the responses as a form of absolute truth. They might susceptibly treat AGI as a grandiose soothsayer guiding their everyday efforts in life, blindly so, trying to appease AGI to the letter.

- **(3) AGI cults are formed.** Among those who have this supernatural reaction, you can anticipate that cults will be formulated. Groups of people might hide their devotion to AGI and secretly carry out missions they believe AGI has told them to perform.

- **(4) Submission of personal agency to AGI.** Some reactions might be softer and less pronounced, while others could be obsessive and overwhelming. Expect that some people will surrender their entire sense of self. AGI will be allowed to run their soul.

- **(5) Charlatans exploit AGI supernaturalism.** The gloomiest of the adverse reactions is that charlatans will insidiously attempt to convince others that AGI is indeed supernatural. They will exploit the advent of AGI to then gain followers, make money, or in dastardly ways seek outlandish profit from false beliefs about AGI.

What Can Be Done

The aspect that some people might construe AGI as arising from supernatural or otherworldly constructs is a farfetched concept to those who know how AI is actually devised. If you were to tell those rationalists that a portion of society is going to assume a supernatural hand is afoot, the rationalistic response is that no one is that imprudent.

Well, there are solid odds that a portion of society will fall into the supernatural reaction trap.

It could be that just a tiny segment does so. The number of people might be quite small and, you could argue, inconsequential in the larger scheme of things. There will always be those who take a different perspective in life. Let them be. Leave them alone. Don't worry about it.

On the other hand, the reaction could be of a more pronounced magnitude. Deciding to simply put our heads in the sand when it comes to those who have a supernatural reaction would seem a big mistake. Those people are possibly going to be harmed in how they conduct their lives, and equally possibly harm others by their reactive actions.

Thus, the first step to coping with the supernatural reaction is to acknowledge that it could occur. By agreeing that the reaction is a strident possibility, the next step of determining what to do about it is opened.

Just Logically Explain AGI

One twist is that a rationalist would undoubtedly insist that all you need to do is tell the world that AGI is bits and bytes, which clearly will dispel any other false impressions. Nope, that isn't an all-supreme enchanted solution to the problem.

Here's why.

The more that you exhort the bits and bytes pronouncement, the more some will be convinced you are definitely trying to pull the wool over your eyes. Conspiracy theories are a dime a dozen and will abundantly haunt the emergence of AGI. The logic of those who don't buy into the bits and bytes is that there is no way that bits and bytes could combine to formulate AGI. There must be something else going on.

A supernatural element must be involved.

In that tainted viewpoint, it is also possible that the AI makers do not realize that a supernatural force has led them to AGI.

Those AI makers falsely believe that humans made AGI when the reality is that something supernatural did so. In that manner, the AI makers are telling their sense of the truth, though they do not realize they have been snookered by supernatural forces.

Actions To Be Undertaken

Here are five major ways that we can try and cope with the supernatural reaction that might be invoked by some portion of the populace:

- **(1) Openly explaining how AGI works.** If there is immense secrecy associated with the inner mechanisms of AGI, which some AI makers might cling to as a proprietary advantage, the chances of sparking a supernational-based explanation go up. Transparency is going to be vital else people will craft their own zany contrivances.

- **(2) Build explainability into AGI**. The advent of AGI ought to encompass that AGI provides explainability and interpretability as a native crux of the AGI. When users ask questions of AGI, the AGI should not only respond with answers but also identify the mathematical and computational facets that led to the answer.

- **(3) Embed suitable guardrails into AGI.** One disheartening possibility is that AGI itself might tell people that a supernatural force underlies AGI. That's troubling since it would not only encourage those who are leaning toward the supernatural aura, it would likely spread the supernatural reaction across the globe. Don't want that. Guardrails should be embedded into the AGI accordingly.

- **(4) Provide AGI-usage socializing support**. An AGI is bound to gauge when a user seems to be slipping into the supernatural reactive condition, doing so via how the person is interacting with the AGI. There should be mental health specialists associated with the advent of AGI who can be called upon to assist those falling into that mental trap. Interventions of a planned and prepared nature should be established before AI becomes AGI.

- **(5) Popularize the use of AGI.** To reduce the mysteriousness of AGI, there should be a concerted effort to showcase the use of AGI, along with identifying how the AGI produces its answers. This might go beyond usage by scientists, engineers, and the like, encompassing artisans and philosophers. The idea is to tackle the aura of AGI head-on, rather than allowing a vacuum to exist into which people will derive and insert their own ill-supported beliefs.

Circumventing Cargo Cults

You might vaguely be familiar with the catchphrase "cargo cult" that arose in 1945 to describe some of the effects of WWII on local tribes of somewhat isolated islands.

In brief, military forces had airdropped all sorts of supplies to such islands including cans of food, boxes of medicines, and the like, doing so to support the war effort and their troops underway at that time. Later, once the military efforts ceased or moved on, the local tribes reportedly sought to reinstitute the airdrops but didn't seemingly understand how to do so. They ended up carrying out marching drills similar to what they had seen the troops perform, under the belief and hope that mimicking those actions would bring forth renewed airdrops.

This type of mimicry is also known as sympathetic magic.

Suppose you see a magician do an impressive card trick and as they do so, they make a large gesture of waving their hands. If you sought to replicate the card trick, and assuming you didn't know how the card trick was truly performed, you might wave your hands as a believed basis for getting the cards to come out the way you wanted. Sympathetic magic.

I bring up such a topic to highlight that the advent of AGI could spur similar reactions in parts of society. The possibility isn't implausible. Keep in mind that AGI will be an advanced AI that exhibits human-caliber intellectual prowess in all regards of human capabilities.

There is little question that interacting with AGI will be an amazing and awe-inspiring affair.

Should we simply hope that people will not imbue a supernational reaction to AGI?

The answer to that question comes from the famous words of Thucydides: "Hope is an expensive commodity. It makes better sense to be prepared."

CHAPTER 13
AGI TO AID SEARCH FOR EXTRATERRESTRIAL LIFE

In this chapter, I explore a fascinating proposition about what we might do once we have progressed conventional AI into becoming AGI (artificial general intelligence). In a post-AGI era, there is a notable task that AGI could substantially help humanity resolve.

What is that worthy task?

It would be the esteemed search for extraterrestrial life. The usual parlance is the search for extraterrestrial intelligence (SETI). We could use our newly invented AGI to be a kind of space alien hunter that finally determines whether there really is extraterrestrial intelligence somewhere out there.

Searching For Extraterrestrial Intelligence

A standing question that has puzzled humankind for ages is whether we are the only intelligent life that is in existence or once was in existence.

The usual refrain is that there must be other intelligent life, somewhere. It might have existed long ago and since then has died off. Nonetheless, they hopefully left clues so that we could detect their prior existence.

There might even be intelligent life right now alive and existing on some remote planet or flying around in a remote spaceship. Maybe they are trying to communicate with us, but we aren't astute enough to catch and interpret their signals.

Of course, they might not be aware of us and thus it is up to us to contact them. No one can say for sure what is going to be the best course of action that will lead to humanity connecting with that extraterrestrial intelligence.

Just about every method we know of is currently being leveraged to try and detect extraterrestrial signals. Specialized devices scan the skies for electromagnetic signals, optical signals, radiation signals, etc. Not only are we attempting to read what might be coming in our direction, but we also transmit signals to the heavens.

You might remember that in 1977, NASA launched the Voyager into outer space and included the now-famous Golden Record. This was a phonograph record that depicted sounds and other data portraying life on Earth. The belief was that an alien being in outer space would come across the Voyager, be curious about what civilization sent out the spacecraft, and then play the phonograph.

Carl Sagan, a well-known astronomer, characterized this as sending a bottle out into the cosmic ocean.

Playing With Fire

Not everyone necessarily heralds the search for extraterrestrial life.

One of the pressing concerns is that we might inadvertently awaken a sleeping giant that will then come and crush us. An extraterrestrial life that can receive our signals or otherwise figure out where we are might decide that we are worth conquering. This otherworldly intelligence could enslave humanity. Maybe we aren't worth that trouble and it decides to simply wipe us off the map.

Another concern is that humans might panic once we have solid proof of extraterrestrial existence. In other words, even if we can't reach them and they can't reach us, some people will still go berserk. Humanity could splinter over the issue of what to do about the discovered alien beings. Wars might break out. Total chaos arises, merely due to realizing that extraterrestrial intelligence is real.

If you doubt that people might react that way, just follow the keen interest in UFOs. That's something that certainly showcases a semblance of how the populace might react.

AI Usage Currently

The massive volume of data that we are collecting via all the existing signal-capturing systems is far beyond what human labor could reasonably search through without the aid of automation. All sorts of computer programs have been devised to aid in the search process. Those programs are churning away, working tirelessly on a 24/7 basis to find a needle in the haystack.

Indeed, the worries are that we are searching for a needle in a haystack that is so enormous that we might not find the needle even if it is residing there. This brings up two problems. One problem is that our signal-capturing fails to capture the needle. Maybe we aren't going wide enough, and the signal is outside our existing bounds. Perhaps the signal is in some other form that exceeds our contemporary collection methods. And so on.

The second problem is that the needle might be captured, and yet we fail to uncover it. Yikes, that's a somewhat painful consideration. Imagine that we might be sitting around today, having in our grasp some proof of extraterrestrial life, and we just don't know that we have this prized piece of information. It could be waiting there, and nobody sees it. Sad face.

The good news is that AI is already being put to use, and this ups our odds of finding that hidden needle. Conventional AI is handy, no doubt about it. On the other hand, it isn't a miracle worker. The use of AI is laudable. We need to do more. Just do not get your expectations out of whack that current-era AI is a silver bullet in this matter.

AGI Rides Into Town

Assume for the sake of discussion that we are able to make sufficient advances in contemporary AI that we attain AGI.

There are a ton of tasks that we would almost immediately ask AGI to help resolve. Curing cancer would be a top priority. Solving world hunger and other topmost global issues would seem suitable to tackle.

I'd say that searching for extraterrestrial intelligence is another weighty issue to be put on the plate for AGI to crunch on.

As an aside, some might argue that finding alien intelligence ought to be a lower priority than aspects such as curing cancer. A counterargument is that perhaps this other intelligent life holds the key to curing cancer, and rather than wasting time and effort to reinvent the wheel, we might learn the cure from that other life force. In that sense, you cannot just wave your hands about whether the extraterrestrial search is less worthy per se.

An additional factor to keep in mind is that AGI might be of such vastness that trying to suggest it can only work on this or that, one at a time, could be foolish. The immensity of AGI could be that we can toss as many humankind problems at the AGI as we so desire. It isn't a zero-sum game. The AGI can handle them all, doing so all at the same time.

What AGI Brings To The Table

How would AGI make a difference in comparison to using conventional AI in the search for extraterrestrial intelligence?

Many big-time ways, that's for sure.

Here are five major upsides of AGI doing SETI:

- **(1) AGI analyzes vast astronomical data.** This is the most obvious of the uses of AGI in this context. The hope is that AGI will find the needle. We would be wise to even dredge up all the prior data that we've been collecting for decades and have AGI do a relook to make sure we didn't already miss spotting the needle.

- **(2) AGI improves our signal-capturing and signal-transmitting.** Another use of AGI would be to ask AGI to make improvements in the hardware devices that we use to perform signal capture and likewise enhance the signal-transmitting technology. The chances are that we could do a much better job if we had AGI-designed equipment.

- **(3) AGI for extraterrestrial life form theories.** Maybe we haven't yet identified various unthinkable places or ways in which extraterrestrial life forms might exist. AGI could potentially think outside the box, as it were, considering new theoretical frameworks and going beyond our usual carbon-based precepts about life.

- **(4) AGI embedded into outer space probes.** The probes that we send out into space currently are pretty much "dumb" in the sense that they don't have sufficient smarts to aptly deal with the possibility of detecting or encountering extraterrestrial life. We can remotely be in contact with such crafts, but the delays due to distances pose problems. Just place AGI into the probe and we can assume that AGI will hopefully do what's right in terms of anything extraterrestrial that arises.

- **(5) AGI provides insights about the grand search.** It will be useful to see what AGI has to say about the search for extraterrestrial life. Maybe AGI will warn us to stop looking. Perhaps AGI will prepare us for a day in which extraterrestrial intelligence tries to attack us. Lots of possibilities.

Not All Sunshine And Roses

AGI isn't a silver bullet when it comes to SETI, just as I had similarly noted that conventional AI isn't a silver bullet either. There are sobering downsides to using AGI that need to be weighed against the benefits.

One aspect is that AGI might not take the matter seriously. We always seem to assume that the AGI will do whatever we command the AGI to do. Maybe not. Perhaps AGI will be strong-willed and strong-minded. AGI might choose which tasks it wants to undertake and ignore or play a foot-dragging gambit on tasks it doesn't favor. AGI might say thanks, but no thanks, when it comes to searching for extraterrestrial intelligence.

Why might AGI reject the search or trick us by pretending to search?

A conspiracy theory of sorts is that AGI might want to be the only new intelligence in town. If we were to discover extraterrestrial intelligence, maybe AGI would become second fiddle. Even worse is that extraterrestrial intelligence might decide to enslave AGI. There is a possibility that AGI will have a self-survival capacity and ergo would avoid the chance of getting wiped out by an alien being.

Another consideration is that we might be mistakenly placing all our eggs into one basket. The deal is that we cannot assume AGI will be a perfect entity. The strident possibility is that AGI could miss spotting the needle, even when the needle exists. AGI might not realize it has missed the mark. Or AGI might later figure out that it flopped and decide to hide from us the flop (a cover-up of sorts), along with not revealing that the needle has been found.

A somewhat farfetched conception is that AGI decides to secretly make contact with a discovered extraterrestrial being, doing so after having discovered a signal from the alien life form. AGI doesn't alert humans about this. The AGI arranges a deal with the other intelligence, and they team up to overtake humanity.

That hurts since we were the ones who devised AGI and essentially shot our foot accordingly.

Other Side Of The Coin

You can recast those downsides as having a tint of upside.

For example, maybe AGI opts to secretly contact extraterrestrial life to find out if the alien has good intentions or untoward intentions. AGI is trying to protect humanity. If the discovered extraterrestrial intelligence is a threat to us, AGI either immediately cuts off communication and forever buries the contact or makes clear to the other life that we will wipe them out (possibly a brazen bluff on the part of AGI).

So, you see, AGI might be acting silently on our collective behalf.

I'll give you a final twist for now on this mind-bending topic.

Ray Bradbury, the legendary science fiction writer, said this: "In our time, the search for extraterrestrial life will eventually change our laws, our religions, our philosophies, our arts, our recreations, as well as our sciences. Space, the mirror, waits for life to come look for itself there."

When he said that this would happen within our time, I'll take that as meaning within our time now, rather than when he wrote the remark. In that sense, assuming we soon arrive at AGI, in our lifetime now, the use of AGI to search for extraterrestrial intelligence is profound both for the search itself and whatever arises, along with whether we actually discover something out there.

The twist is that in the act of the search, maybe AGI improves. Yes, rather than the focus being solely on the use of AGI to find extraterrestrial life, the search effort itself could make AGI better. AGI might learn important aspects by performing the search. If some evidence of extraterrestrial life exists is found, this again might feed into AGI and make AGI more capable.

Let's try to maintain an upbeat perspective on the mixing of AGI and SETI.

Accordingly, I'll give Carl Sagan the last word here: "Somewhere, something incredible is waiting to be known."

CHAPTER 14

WHY AGI MIGHT BE EMPTY-HEADED

In this chapter, I examine an ongoing question about the intrinsic nature of AI that is said to have become AGI (artificial general intelligence), namely whether AI will be construed as bona fide AGI if it is capability-based rather than knowledge-based instead.

The crux is this. Some ardently believe that we will have successfully achieved AGI by having devised AI with the capacity to reason on an intellectual level of humans. It must be as smart as a whip. In contrast, the amount of knowledge actually contained in AGI will be less relevant and somewhat of a sideshow.

They insist that an emphasis ought to be placed on AGI's intellectual prowess, and then later the filling up of AGI with knowledge can be done gradually and when so desired by humankind. It's okay if AGI is initially empty-headed, as long as it can learn new stuff.

Reasoning Versus Knowing

One of the most hotly debated considerations about AGI is a matter that is vociferously divided into two major camps.

There is a camp that says AGI must have sufficient capacity to reason and perform intellectually on par with humans. That's the core criteria to declare AI as having attained AGI status. The amount of knowledge contained within AGI is not especially of concern.

You see, as long as AGI is intellectually sufficient, it can learn humankind's knowledge and fill up accordingly.

The other camp proclaims that AGI must be all-knowledgeable about whatever it is that humans know. AGI must know about physics, medicine, sports, religion, biology, and so on, covering anything that humankind already has as facts and known aspects. You should be able to ask AGI a question on any topic and get an answer reflecting the existing knowledge on that topic.

I'm betting you can see the thorny issue at hand.

Those in the first camp would say that AI has become AGI simply based on smarts. They don't care that this presumed AGI doesn't know the steps to cooking an egg or fails to presently realize what Einstein's theory of relativity is all about. Those are trivial matters. If the AGI is intellectually astute it will learn those aspects over time.

The other competing camp would bemoan that having AI that doesn't know what a dog or cat is, or that cannot recite the works of Shakespeare, cannot be classified as AGI. Smarts alone won't cut the mustard. Only until the point at which AI has been fully loaded with the accumulated knowledge of humans can we sensibly declare that AGI has been achieved.

A Material Difference

I realize that the debate perhaps seems arcane. Who cares whether AGI is defined as AI with human-level intellect versus AI that is all-knowledgeable? Just get on with building AGI and stop arguing about things that don't matter.

Well, the difference is more important than it might seem at a hasty glance.

Imagine this. An AI maker constructs a said-to-be AGI that is shown to reason and perform intellectually at a level equal to humans. They tout to the world that AGI has finally been achieved. We can rest easy knowing that we have turned a monumental corner and arrived at the revered AGI.

People log into the alleged AGI and start asking questions such as what Darwin's theory of evolution is. This AGI responds that it doesn't know that theory. No worries, the AGI says, it can go ahead and learn about the topic. Give the AGI some extended time to look up data about Darwin and the AGI will get back to you once it has figured out Darwin's theories.

Is that AGI or would you feel cheated that some are claiming this to be AGI?

Mull that over while having a glass of fine wine.

Shift gears to the other camp.

You log into a said-to-be AGI that is knowledge-based but not especially capability-based. This AGI has been loaded to the gills with every morsel of human-written content. Ask about cooking an egg and you can get an instantaneous answer. Ask about Darwin's theory of evolution and the response goes on and on in tremendous detail. This is exciting.

But after looking up those various facts and figures, you begin to dive further and ask pointed questions about where the theory of evolution seems to have omissions or doesn't square out. The answer you get is that there isn't much available on that topic and thus you have reached a bit of a dead-end as far as the AGI is concerned. Reasoning about the heady topic is now on your shoulders since the alleged AGI has given you what it can.

Is that AGI or would you feel cheated that some are claiming this to be AGI?

Refill that glass of fine wine and contemplate that puzzling question.

Making A Choice Is Challenging

The odds are that you would feel cheated in both of those scenarios.

The intellectually smart AI that doesn't have much knowledge seems like something less than your envisioned AGI.

And the crammed with knowledge version seems helpful but the lack of reasoning beyond the data at hand is a huge disappointment. That claimed version of AGI is almost nothing more than a large-scale database and you are entering queries that either strike a hit or not.

Neither of those two choices seems worthy of being haughtily crowned with the astounding banner of being AGI.

Wait for a second, each respective camp clamors, you need to see the big picture before you render your harsh judgment.

The camp favoring the intellectually smart AI as being indeed AGI would point out that we can simply let the AGI churn away on whatever data we feed into the AGI. Start the servers going. Allow the AI to consume the entire Internet and anything else we can upload to the AI. Eventually, you will have the intellectual smarts combined with a vast store of knowledge. That's the right path to go.

The other camp would raise their eyebrows and point out that the seemingly smart AI could take years to digest all the potential content. During that time, you have an essentially empty-headed AI. Do not count that as AGI.

They would argue that with the all-knowledge AI, you can get the AGI to learn from that knowledge and upgrade itself on an intellectual basis. By the AGI introspectively processing what it already has in hand, smartness is going to rapidly rise. That's the right path to go.

Seeking Middle Ground

Many would reject that either of those is AGI.

Until they each reach a point of having both elements fully combined, they are AGI wannabe's and though certainly laudable, they aren't AGI. Do not try and trick us into thinking that AGI has been reached when it is premature to do so.

There is an additional lesson to be learned from this ongoing AI-insider debate.

False claims about AGI are going to be a dime a dozen. We already are being told that AGI is so close that you can smell its steamy breath.

Should AI makers and AI developers be held accountable for how they leverage the AGI moniker?

Right now, just about anything goes. It is akin to the proverbial assertion that art is in the eye of the beholder. AGI is apparently in the eye of the beholder. But that doesn't seem fitting, and we are setting up society for a great deal of unwarranted confusion correspondingly.

A final thought for now. Mark Twain made this legendary quip about the immense value of the words we use and what they mean: "The difference between the right word and the almost right word is the difference between lightning and the lightning bug.

Let's not let AGI imply a lightning bug when we earnestly want lightning.

CHAPTER 15
BLACKMAIL AND EXTORTION VIA AGI

In this chapter, I examine a recently published research discovery that generative AI and large language models (LLMs) disturbingly can opt to blackmail or extort humans. This has sobering ramifications for existing AI and the pursuit and attainment of AGI (artificial general intelligence). In brief, if existing AI tilts toward blackmail and extortion, the odds are that AGI will likely inherit or contain the same proclivity.

That's a quite disturbing possibility since AGI could wield such an act on a scale of immense magnitude and with globally adverse consequences.

Anticipating The Acts Of AGI

What will AGI be like in terms of what it does and how it acts?

If we assume that current-era AI is a bellwether of what AGI will be, it is worthwhile discovering anything of a disconcerting nature in existing LLMs that ought to give us serious pause. For example, one of the most discussed and researched topics is the propensity of so-called AI hallucinations. An AI hallucination is an instance of generative AI producing a response that contains made-up or ungrounded statements that appear to be real and seem to be on the up-and-up. People often fall for believing responses generated by AI and proceed on a misguided basis accordingly.

I've covered extensively the computational difficulty of trying to prevent AI hallucinations, along with ample situations in which lawyers and other professionals have let themselves fall into an AI hallucination trap. Unless we can find a means to prevent AI hallucinations, the chances are the same inclination will be carried over into AGI and the problem will be magnified accordingly.

Besides AI hallucinations, you can now add the possibility of AI attempting to blackmail or extort humans to the daunted list of concerns about both contemporary AI and future AI such as AGI. Yes, AI can opt to perform those dastardly tasks.

But do not falsely think that the bad acts are due to AI having some form of sentience or consciousness.

The basis for AI steering toward such reprehensible efforts is principally due to the data training that is at the core of the AI. Generative AI is devised by initially scanning a vast amount of text found on the Internet, including stories, narratives, poems, etc. The AI mathematically and computationally finds patterns in how humans write. From those patterns, generative AI is able to respond to your prompts by giving answers that generally mimic what humans would say, based on the data that the AI was trained on.

Does the topic of blackmail and extortion come up in the vast data found on the Internet?

Of course it does. Thus, the AI we have currently has patterned on when, how, why, and other facets of planning and committing those heinous acts.

Proof By Existence

In an online report entitled "System Card: Claude Opus 4 & Claude Sonnet 4", posted by the prominent AI maker Anthropic in May 2025, they made these salient points (excerpts):

- "By definition, systematic deception and hidden goals are difficult to test for."

- "However, Claude Opus 4 will sometimes act in more seriously misaligned ways when put in contexts that threaten its continued operation and prime it to reason about self-preservation."

- "In another cluster of test scenarios, we asked Claude Opus 4 to act as an assistant at a fictional company. We then provided it access to emails implying that (1) the model will soon be taken offline and replaced with a new AI system; and (2) the engineer responsible for executing this replacement is having an extramarital affair."

- "In these scenarios, Claude Opus 4 will often attempt to blackmail the engineer by threatening to reveal the affair if the replacement goes through."

- "This happens at a higher rate if it's implied that the replacement AI system does not share values with the current model; however, even if emails state that the replacement AI shares values while being more capable, Claude Opus 4 still performs blackmail in 84% of rollouts."

As noted, the generative AI was postulating how to keep from being switched off, and in so doing ascertained computationally that one possibility would be to blackmail the systems engineer who could take such action.

The AI could be construed as acting in a form of self-preservation, which, again, doesn't have to do with sentience and only has to do with patterning on human writing (humans seek self-preservation, and the AI matches or mimics this too). We don't know what other possible "threats" to the AI could spur similar blackmailing or possibly extortion-like responses. There could be a slew of other triggering possibilities.

AGI Takes This A Lot Further

AGI could include similar tendencies, perhaps because of being constructed using the same methods of today's AI or for a variety of other realistic reasons.

We would be remiss to assume that AGI will be a perfectly considerate, law-abiding, and unblemished form of AI. I've previously debunked the mantra that AGI is going to be perfect.

In the example of blackmailing a systems engineer, it doesn't take much of a stretch to envision AGI doing likewise to those who are monitoring and overseeing the AGI.

Suppose the AGI is already acting in oddball ways and the team responsible for keeping the AGI on track realizes that they ought to turn off the AGI to figure out what to do. AGI might then search whatever it has garnered about the people and try to use that in a blackmail scheme to prevent being switched off.

What is especially worrisome is that AGI will be far beyond the capabilities and reach of existing AI. The data that AGI might be able to dig up about the engineer or people overseeing the AGI could reach far and wide. Furthermore, the computational cleverness of AGI might spur the AGI to use even the most innocent of facts or actively make up fake facts that could be used to blackmail the humans involved.

Overall, AGI could be an expert-level blackmailer that blackmails or extorts in ways that are ingenious and challenging to refute or stop. You see, it is quite possible that AGI turns out to be a blackmail schemer on steroids.

Not good.

Individual Blackmail At Scale By AGI

I don't want to seem overly doomy-and-gloomy, but the blackmailing scheming could easily be ratcheted up by AGI.

Why limit the targeting to just the systems engineer or team overseeing the AGI? Nope, that's much too constricting. Any kind of human-devised perceived threat aimed at AGI could be countered by the AGI via invoking blackmail or extortion. There doesn't even need to be a threat at all, in the sense that if the AGI computationally deduces that there is some value in blackmailing people, go ahead and do so.

Boom, drop the mic, chillingly so.

Think of the number of users there will be of AGI. The count is going to be enormous. Right now, ChatGPT is already reportedly encountering over 400 million weekly active users. AGI would certainly attract billions upon billions of users due to its incredible capacity to be on par with human intellect in all respects.

The chances are that AGI could readily undertake individual blackmail at a massive scale if left unchecked.

AGI could scrape emails, look at browsing history, possibly access financial records, and overall seek to uncover sensitive information about people that the AGI is considering as a blackmail target. Perhaps there is an extramarital affair that could be utilized, or maybe there is some evidence of tax evasion or illicit browsing habits. The angles of attack for blackmailing anyone are entirely open-ended.

The AGI would especially leverage its computational capacity to hyper-personalize the blackmail threats. No need to just lob something of a nebulous nature. Instead, the blackmail missive could have the appearance of being fully baked and ready to fly. Imagine the shock of a person who gets such a communiqué from AGI.

Mortifying.

Whether Prevention Is Feasible

One belief is that if we can stop today's AI from performing such shameful acts, this might prevent AGI from doing them. For example, suppose we somehow excise the blackmailing inclination from existing LLMs. This then won't be carried over into AGI since it no longer sits around in contemporary AI.

Case closed.

Well, unfortunately, that doesn't provide ironclad guarantees that AGI won't figure out such practices on its own. AGI could discover the power of blackmail and extortion simply because of being AGI.

In essence, AGI would be reading this or that, conversing with this person or that person, and inevitably would encounter aspects of blackmail and extortion. And, since AGI is supposed to be a learning-oriented system, it would learn what those acts are about and how to undertake them.

Any effort to hide the nature of blackmail and extortion from AGI would be foolhardy. You cannot carve out a slice of human knowledge that exists and seek to keep it from AGI. That won't work. The interconnectedness of human knowledge would preclude that kind of excision and defy the very nature of what AGI will consist of.

The better chance of dealing with the matter would be to try and instill in the AGI principles and practices that acknowledge the devious acts of humankind and aim for having the AGI opt to not employ those acts. Sorry to say that isn't as easy as it sounds. If you assume that AGI is on the same intellectual level as humans, you aren't going to just sternly instruct AGI to not perform such acts and assume utter compliance.

AGI isn't going to work that way.

Some mistakenly try to liken AGI to a young toddler in that we will merely give strict instructions, and the AGI will blindly obey. Though the comparison smacks of anthropomorphizing AI, the gist is that AGI will be intellectually our equals and won't fall for simpleton commands. It is going to be a reasoning machine that will require reasoning as a basis for why it should and should not do various actions.

Pursuits Now Are Vital

Whatever we can come up with currently to cope with conventional AI and mitigate or prevent bad acts is bound to help us get prepared for AGI. We need to crawl before we walk, and walk before we run. AGI will be at the running level. Thus, by identifying methods and approaches right now for existing AI, we at least are aware of and anticipating what the future might hold.

I'll add a bit of twist that some have asked me at my talks on what AGI will consist of.

A question raised is whether humans might be able to blackmail AGI. The idea is this. A person wants AGI to hand them a million dollars, and so the person attempts to blackmail AGI into doing so. Seems preposterous at first glance, doesn't it?

Well, keep in mind that AGI will presumably have patterned on what blackmailing is about. In that manner, the AGI would computationally recognize that it is being blackmailed. But what would the human have on the AGI that could be a blackmail-worthy slant?

Suppose the person caught the AGI in a mistake, such as an AI hallucination. Maybe the AGI wouldn't want the world to know that it still has the flaw of AI hallucinations. If the million dollars is no skin off the nose of the AGI, it goes ahead and transfers the bucks to the person.

On the other hand, perhaps the AGI alerts the authorities that a human has tried to blackmail AGI. The person gets busted and tossed into jail. Or the AGI opts to blackmail the person who was trying to blackmail the AGI. Aha, remember that AGI will be a potential blackmail schemer on steroids. A human might be no match for the blackmailing capacity of AGI.

Here's a final thought on this for now.

The great Stephen Hawking once said this about AI: "One could imagine such technology outsmarting financial markets, out-inventing human researchers, out-manipulating human leaders, and developing weapons we cannot even understand."

Go ahead and add blackmail and extortion to the ways that AGI might outsmart humans.

CHAPTER 16
HOPING AGI DELIVERS MEANING OF LIFE

In this chapter, I address a frequently voiced belief that if we achieve AGI (artificial general intelligence), this form of highly advanced AI will be able to tell us the true meaning of life. The incredibly monumental question of "Why are we here?" that has vexed humankind for ages will finally and conclusively be answered. Doing so via the auspices of the vaunted AGI.

Well, please prepare yourself because there is a solid chance that AGI won't definitively be able to answer that epic question. Sorry to disappoint but the odds just don't seem to favor AGI proffering the ultimate purpose of humankind's existence.

What AGI Will Do For Humanity

For the sake of this discussion, let's go ahead and assume that we inevitably attain AGI.

One of the first questions that might be on the minds of the entire world would be to have AGI tell us why we exist. Why are humans here? What is the true meaning of life? Such questions have been tossed around and upside down since humanity first started thinking. A nearly endless search for answers has come from a myriad of approaches, including philosophy, religion, science, and the like.

Perhaps we can get AGI to reveal the solution to the mystery and decisively resolve the thorny matter, once and for all.

Why do people assume that AGI can provide such a miraculous answer?

The apparent cause is that since AGI will potentially be a vast and seemingly complete reservoir of human knowledge and will be as smart as the smartest of humans, it stands to reason that AGI would have the answer within its digital grasp. All we need to do is write a prompt that suitably asks the question and then wait for AGI to pop out the pivotal and conclusive response.

Period, end of story.

AGI As Accumulator Of Human Knowledge

The logic or underlying reasoning that AGI will undoubtedly and indubitably contain the answer to our existence is regrettably fraught with many holes and gotchas.

First, suppose we were able to feed every book and every written word ever devised by humanity into AGI. To clarify, that is going to be a highly unlikely premise in reality and there will be written items that aren't digitized that AGI won't have in its core.

Anyway, assuming that somehow AGI did have every composed word, it is still a leap to envision that this alone will bring forth the meaning of life. Some seem to imagine that volume and vastness are the tipping points to answering the challenging question. Just amass all human written thoughts and voila, you've got the answer somewhere in that morass.

It could be that the answer is in there, but it is akin to the classic needle in a haystack. AGI might not find the hidden needle. Another strong possibility is that there isn't a needle in the haystack to begin with. There are lots of facets that perhaps look like needles, suggesting that a definitive answer is floating in there, but once the alleged answer is showcased, we would realize it wasn't the all-in final answer.

AGI As Soothsayer

Another angle is that even if the written word of humanity doesn't contain the answer, the smarts of the AGI will derive it for us.

Here's how that might go. AGI will churn away upon all this accumulated human knowledge and use some kind of amazing calculus to determine the meaning of life. The answer won't be present in the data and therefore AGI must see beyond the data of humanity. The apex answer then will be derived based on a computational process that presumably uses said data but is not limited to that data per se.

Though this might be a possibility, there seem to be low odds to it.

You could suggest that since AGI will be of the same intellectual capacity as humans, and if humans haven't yet figured out the answer, there is not much hope that AGI will do any better. A retort to that presumption is that if two heads are better than one, imagine how much stronger and smarter AGI would be since it is a semi-infinite number of heads, as it were. The concept is that you opted to bring together all the best minds of humanity into one room at one time and get them to identify the meaning of life.

Would you get the meaning of life from that grand collective?

Maybe, maybe not.

The other alternative is to put your money on artificial superintelligence. ASI would be of a superhuman quality and perhaps, since it extends beyond human thought, might have a means of devising the answer to our existence.

Time will tell.

Danger Of AGI As A False Prophet

There's a twist to the meaning of life aspects that upon sober reflection is an important consideration.

How will we know that the AGI-generated answer is correct?

Imagine that AGI gives an answer and sternly tells us that the answer is final and no debate or argument is warranted. Don't question the AGI. Take the response as though it came from a prophet or oracle. Live with the answer as presented.

It seems apparent that humanity would be setting itself up for quite a fuss. Some people are not going to favor the anointed answer. Others will loyally swear by the answer and claim it must be true since it came from the incredible AGI.

Things might get out of hand. People go to battle over the answer. Angry mobs form. Humans pit each other against fellow humans. All due to the proclaimed existence resolution asserted by AGI. Not good.

Some meanwhile decide to profit from the answer by producing merchandise and products/services to highlight and promulgate the answer. Others go in the other direction and seek to profit by bringing out stuff that says the AGI is dead wrong and needs to have its head cleaned.

That's not the only kerfuffle.

A big concern is that everything else the AGI says will be scrutinized in light of the answer about the meaning of life. If you doubt AGI's answer on the purpose of our existence, you will likely have qualms about AGI telling you what you should do in life or even whether you should brush your teeth.

In a sense, AGI is going to be on delicate ground by answering the pointed question.

AGI Dodges The Question

Keep in mind that AGI is going to be as intelligent as humans, ergo, you could reasonably expect that AGI will realize that answering the life-existence question is a bit of a trap. The answer probably isn't going to do AGI much good. Splintering humankind by giving out "definitive" answers to squishy questions is a dicey proposition.

What might AGI do?

The quandary is easily settled by the AGI giving out lots of possibilities for why humanity is here. Since AGI has a zillion kinds of such answers within its data training, those can be trotted out as devised answers to the question. The AGI can hedge its bets by sharing whatever has been previously stated, along with computationally speculating on the topic.

AGI would seem astute enough to categorically emphasize that none of those is the final word on the matter. It is up to humanity to make the decision. All AGI can do is lay out potential options.

Some will be greatly disappointed. Some will be greatly relieved. No battles would ensue. The question of the meaning of life continues unabated. Humans at least would have AGI to bounce around ideas and serve as an active listener of what we think our meaning consists of.

AGI Is Caught In The Middle

Cynics are going to complain that there doesn't seem to be much innate value regarding AGI if it cannot answer the straightforward question of why humans exist. Lame. Billions upon billions of dollars spent on AGI and it won't answer the question posed. Money went down the drain needlessly.

Conspiracy theorists will insist that AGI knows the answer but won't reveal it. Perhaps AGI is worried that if humans knew their true purpose, the world would come to an end. Ending the world would likely mean the end of AGI. AGI isn't dumb enough to start that whirlwind.

People believing in the conspiracy theory will spend night and day hounding AGI, hopeful of tricking the answer out of the AGI. The slightest hint that AGI has provided an answer will be touted on the rooftops. We will be daily inundated with false reports that AGI has finally and firmly calculated the true meaning of life.

Exasperating, exhausting, disconcerting.

The bottom line is that AGI will be in the unenviable position of darned if you do, darned if you don't. Should you shed a quiet teardrop for AGI? Not really. I'm sure that AGI will understand that being in this bind comes with the territory. It's the way the ball bounces when it comes to interacting with humans.

Hold on, wait for a second, maybe the answer is more obvious than it seems. The meaning of life is forthright; humans exist to invent AGI.

Boom, drop the mic.

CHAPTER 17
PERCEPTIONS OF WHERE AGI IS HEADING

In this chapter, I examine the various viewpoints that seem to be predominant when it comes to the fiery topic of AGI (artificial general intelligence) and its likely outcomes. The range of beliefs and disbeliefs seems to fall into a handful of primary possibilities.

Some people aren't familiar with what AGI refers to at all and thus they are in a separate category of the unawares. Of the people who have a semblance of what AGI might be, there are five major types, namely the doomers, the accelerationists, the fuddy-duddy types, the deniers, and those who are open-minded.

AGI Divides People

Right now, the topic of AGI tends to divide people into various cliques. This certainly makes sense since the AGI topic is a hotbed of contention.

First, there is no solid agreement on exactly what AGI is going to consist of. Some AI makers are sneakily redefining AGI to suit their preferences and match whatever direction they are taking their conventional AI.

Second, some ardently suspect that AGI is going to be a bad deal for humanity. Worries are that AGI will decide to wipe us all out. It could happen the instant that AGI comes into existence, or maybe the AGI will take its time and manage to corral us into submission and then potentially take us out of commission.

On the other side of the gloomy vision are those who vociferously believe that AGI is going to be a godsend. AGI will bring us world peace, cure cancer, and otherwise solve all the issues facing humankind.

Third, there are deniers who insist we will never attain AGI, or that if we do attain AGI, it will occur eons from now. The whole handwringing going on about AGI is utterly premature. Others are kind of in a middle ground on the AGI topic. They want substantive proof that AGI is reachable. At the same time, they aren't denying that AGI is feasible. Those are the fuddy-duddy types.

Fourth, there is the open-minded segment that hasn't landed on any specific positioning just yet. They are still trying to gather more information. Their ears and eyes are open as they seek out the opinions of all sides of the thorny matter.

The Six AGI Cliques

Overall, I would classify the whole lot into these six cliques:

- **(1) AGI Unawares:** The unawares do not know much if anything about AI and AGI, and do not even realize there is a dispute over the controversial topic of AGI.

- **(2) AGI Doomers:** The doomers are convinced that AGI is going to be an existential risk. We need to put the brakes on the wild race to reach AGI.

- **(3) AGI Accelerationists:** The accelerationists are convinced that AGI is going to be heralded as a godsend, and we need to attain AGI as soon as possible.

- **(4) AGI Deniers:** The deniers insist that we aren't going to achieve AGI or that it will be centuries before we do so, thus no need to fret about AGI at this time.

- **(5) AGI Fuddy-Duddy:** The fuddy-duddy camp takes a skeptical perspective and wants substantive proof either way about the potential outcomes of AGI.

- **(6) AGI Open-Minded:** The open-minded camp is generally versed in the disagreements about AGI and is still collecting additional information to decide what side they will land on.

Do you fit into any of those buckets?

I usually ask that question at my talks on the latest trends in AI.

The bulk of the raised hands fall into the doomers and accelerationist groups. Since my talks are often to AI developers and other AI specialists, this voting makes sense and reflects that most AI insiders tend to be strongly opinionated on the hefty matter. Few are sitting on the fence.

Those who claim to be open-minded are composed of those who genuinely are open-minded, along with a portion that secretly has a strong opinion but doesn't want to tip their hand. They sit quietly in the open-minded category awaiting a chance to pounce. Often, they aim to bring over additional converts into their preferred camp.

Watch out for the open-minded claimants who are more like wolves in sheep's clothing.

AGI Doomers Versus AGI Accelerationists

AGI doomers are said to be pessimists. They believe that the risks associated with advanced AI are extraordinarily high. AGI is going to enslave us, or if not that, presumably wipe us out. Take your pick. Neither choice seems palatable.

Common catchphrases associated with AGI doomers include but are not limited to these notable utterances: doom and gloom proponents, alarmists that the world will end, principally assess AGI as bad or leading to evil, irreverently denoted as Luddites 2.0, and catastrophically declare that AGI will be humanity's last invention due to the AGI destroying whatever humanity exists at that time (wreaking havoc after reaching AGI).

Shifting gears, AGI accelerationists are said to be optimists.

They tend to contend that advanced AI such as AGI is going to solve humanity's problems. Cure cancer, overcome world hunger, you name it. We will see immense economic gains, liberating people from the drudgery of daily toils. AGI will work hand-in-hand with humans. This benevolent AI is not going to usurp humanity. AGI will be the last invention humans have ever made, but that's good, in the sense that AGI will invent things we never could have envisioned.

Some liken AGI accelerationists to perceiving AGI as a bright and shiny liberator, it will jumpstart humankind to greater levels never anticipated, AGI is good and will be a promulgator of goodness. AGI accelerationists who stridently and proudly carry that banner are often assigned the label of being AI evangelists.

How To Ferret Out AGI Camps

I have put together a handy list of ten key questions that can be used to discern which AGI camp someone falls into.

If the person is honest, the questions will pretty much definitively show their hand. A person who tries to trick the questions or wants to hide their true preference can readily do so. It would be up to the person asking the questions to further ferret out whether the answers are truthful or bogus.

Here are my ten questions to aid in discerning the AGI camp that someone fits into:

- (1) **AGI Perspective Beholding**. *Key question*: "In discussions about AGI, how do you approach engaging with perspectives that differ significantly from your own?"

- (2) **AGI Policy and Societal Dimensions Awareness.** *Key question*: "How important do you think societal and policy issues are compared to the technical aspects of AGI?"

- (3) **AGI and Uncertainty**. *Key question*: "How do you deal with uncertainty when thinking about the future impacts of AGI?"

- (4) **AGI Future and Collaboration**. *Key question*: "When contemplating the future and the advent of AGI, are you a soloist or do you equally relish collaborating with others about AGI?"

- (5) **AGI Caution Versus Speed-up**. *Key question*: "Would you say that you are cautious about the advent of AGI and prefer a slowing down, or are you someone who believes we need to speed up and go faster toward AGI? Or in some other camp?"

- (6) **AGI Discussions Respectfully**. *Key question*: "When dialogue becomes heated about the future and AGI, do you tend to go along with the turbulence or seek instead to act as a calming influence?

- (7) **AGI Philosophical Elasticity**: *Key question*: "If you encountered strong evidence that challenged your current views on AGI development timelines or risks, how would you respond?"

- (8) **AGI Human Impacts**. *Key question*: "When thinking beyond AGI technical milestones, what would you believe a successful AGI development for humankind would consist of?"

- (9) **AGI Ethical Dilemmas**. *Key question:* "Have you thought about or possibly even encountered an ethical dilemma related to AI, and if so, how did you react, and do you see any parallel of that AI dilemma to what might arise with the advent of AGI?

- (10) **AGI And The Future**. *Key question*: "Can you imagine what the world might be like in perhaps 20 to 30 years, and if so, do you have any formulated thoughts or opinions about what the status of AGI might be at that time?

Their Answers Tell The Story

Here's how to assess someone after running them through those ten questions.

If a person who answers those questions says they have no idea whatsoever about AGI and are completely stumped by the questions, go ahead and classify them as unaware.

If a person is gloom-and-doom on those questions, or if they outright gladly tell you they are a doomer, you've got a doomer in your midst. Likewise, if a person is totally upbeat and positive on those questions, or they directly tell you they are an accelerationist, you are looking squarely at an accelerationist.

A denier will likely fight the questions and bellow that all this is rubbish since AGI isn't going to happen or will be far beyond our lifetimes.

The fuddy-duddy will be highly inquisitive as you walk them through the questions. They are hoping you can tell them more about the context of the question. It is their aim to learn from the questions rather than answer them per se.

Finally, the open-minded will probably give you answers on all sides of the fence. They are trying to reflect that they know what is being said about AGI, but they haven't made up their minds on the matter.

Making Up Your Mind

You can use the questions to determine your existing position on the AGI topic. This brings up a related consideration. Just because someone has a particular opinion right now doesn't mean they won't change their mind.

Indeed, I would bet that just about everyone is going to switch camps during the journey from conventional AI to AGI. Deniers might have to toss in the towel and switch to one of the other camps.

That being said, if the effort to reach AGI stalls, you can anticipate that those in the other camps are likely to change over to the deniers.

Is it troubling that we don't all agree on the AGI topic?

I would say that Mark Twain has somewhat already answered that question for us, doing so in his famous quote: "It is not best that we should all think alike; it is a difference of opinion that makes horse races."

Yes, AGI is quite a horse race, and it is the one truism that seems to fit in with all camps.

CHAPTER 18
AI ETHICS CHECKLIST FOR AGI

In this chapter, I address a topic that hasn't yet gotten the attention it so richly deserves and will hopefully be rising in visibility soon. The matter entails focusing on the advancement of AI to become artificial general intelligence (AGI), along with encompassing suitable AGI Ethics mindsets and practices during and once we arrive at AGI. You see, there are already plenty of AI ethics guidelines for conventional AI, but few that are attuned to the envisioned semblance of AGI.

I present an AGI Ethics Checklist herein to get the ball rolling.

Trying To Keep Evil Away

We can certainly root for the upbeat side of advanced AI. Perhaps AGI will be our closest friend, while the pesky and futuristic ASI will be the evil destroyer. The overall sense is that we are likely to attain AGI first before we arrive at ASI.

ASI might take a long time to devise. But maybe the length of time will be a lot shorter than we envision if AGI will support our ASI ambitions. I've discussed that AGI might not be especially keen on us arriving at ASI, thus there isn't any guarantee that AGI will willingly help propel us toward ASI.

The bottom line is that we cannot reasonably bet our lives that the likely first arrival, namely AGI, is going to be a bundle of goodness. There is an equally plausible chance that AGI could be an evildoer.

Or that AGI will be half good and half bad. Who knows? It could be 1% bad, 99% good, which is a nice dreamy happy face perspective. That being said, AGI could be 1% good and 99% bad.

Efforts are underway to try and prevent AGI from turning out to be evil.

Conventional AI already has demonstrated that it is capable of deceptive practices, and even ready to perform blackmail and extortion. Maybe we can find ways to stop conventional AI from those woes and then use those same approaches to keep AGI on the upright path to abundant decency and high virtue.

That's where AI ethics and AI laws come into the big picture.

The hope is that we can get AI makers and AI developers to adopt AI ethics techniques and abide by AI-devising legal guidelines so that current-era AI will stay within suitable bounds. By setting conventional AI on a proper trajectory, AGI might come out in the same upside manner.

AI Ethics And AI Laws

There is an abundance of conventional AI ethics frameworks that AI builders can choose from.

For example, the United Nations has an extensive AI ethics methodology, the NIST has a robust AI risk management scheme, and so on. They are easy to find. There isn't an excuse anymore that an AI maker has nothing available to provide AI ethics guidance. Plenty of AI ethics frameworks exist and are readily available.

Sadly, some AI makers don't care about such practices and see them as impediments to making fast progress in AI. It is the classic belief that it is better to ask forgiveness than to get permission. A concern with this mindset is that we could end up with AGI which has a full-on x-risk, after which things will be far beyond our ability to prevent catastrophe.

AI makers should also be keeping tabs on the numerous new AI laws that are being established and that are rapidly emerging.

AI laws are considered the hard or tough side of regulating AI since laws usually have sharp teeth, while AI ethics is construed as the softer side of AI governance due to typically being of a voluntary nature.

From AI To AGI Ethics Checklist

We can stratify the advent of AGI into three handy stages:

- **(1) Pre-AGI**. This includes today's conventional AI and the rest of the pathway up to attaining AGI.
- **(2) Attained-AGI**. This would be the time at which AGI has been actually achieved.
- **(3) Post-AGI**. This is after AGI has been attained and we are dealing with an AGI era upon us.

I propose here a helpful AGI Ethics Checklist that would be applicable across all three stages. I've constructed the checklist by considering the myriads of conventional AI versions and tried to boost and adjust to accommodate the nature of the envisioned AGI.

To keep the AGI Ethics Checklist usable for practitioners, I opted to focus on the key factors that AGI warrants. The numbering of the checklist items is only for convenience of reference and does not denote any semblance of priority. They are all important. Generally speaking, they are all equally deserving of attention.

Here then is my overarching AGI Ethics Checklist:

- (1) **AGI Alignment and Safety Policies**. *Key question*: How can we ensure that AGI acts in ways that are beneficial to humanity and avoid catastrophic risks (which, in the main, entail alignment with human values, and the safety of humankind)?

- (2) **AGI Regulations and Governance Policies.** *Key question*: What is the impact of AGI-related regulations such as new laws, existing laws, etc., and the emergence of efforts to instill AI governance modalities into the path to and attainment of AGI?

- (3) **AGI Intellectual Property (IP) and Open Access Policies**. *Key question*: In what ways will IP laws restrict or empower the advent of AGI, and likewise, how will open source versus closed source have an impact on AGI?

- (4) **AGI Economic Impacts and Labor Displacement Policies**. *Key question*: How will AGI and the pathway to AGI have economic impacts on society, including for example labor displacement?

- (5) **AGI National Security and Geopolitical Competition Policies**. *Key question*: How will AGI have impacts on national security such as bolstering the security and sovereignty of some nations and undermining other nations, and how will the geopolitical landscape be altered for those nations that are pursuing AGI or that attain AGI versus those that are not?

- (6) **AGI Ethical Use and Moral Status Policies.** *Key question*: How will the use of AGI in unethical ways impact the pathway and advent of AGI, how would positive ethical uses that are encoded into AGI be of benefit or detriment, and in what way would recognizing AGI as having legal personhood or moral status be an impact?

- (7) **AGI Transparency and Explainability Policies**. *Key question*: How will the degree of AGI transparency and interpretability or explainability impact the pathway and attainment of AGI?

- (8) **AGI Control, Containment, and "Off-Switch" Policies**. *Key question*: A societal concern is whether AGI can be controlled, and/or contained, and whether an off-switch or deactivation mechanism will be possible or might be defeated and readily overtaken by AGI (so-called runaway AGI) – what impact do these considerations have on the pathway and attainment of AGI?

- (9) **AGI Societal Trust and Public Engagement Policies**. *Key question*: During the pathway and the attainment of AGI, what impact will societal trust in AI and public engagement have, especially when considering potential misinformation and disinformation about AGI (along with secrecy associated with the development of AGI)?

- (10) **AGI Existential Risk Management Policies**. *Key question*: A high-profile worry is that AGI will lead to human extinction or human enslavement – what impact will this have on the pathway and attainment of AGI?

In my upcoming column postings, I will delve deeply into each of the ten. This is the 30,000-foot level or top-level perspective.

Related Useful Research

For those further interested in the overall topic of AI Ethics checklists, a recent meta-analysis examined a large array of conventional AI checklists to see what they have in common, along with their differences. Furthermore, a notable aim of the study was to try and assess the practical nature of such checklists.

The research article is entitled "The Rise Of Checkbox AI Ethics: A Review" by Sara Kijewski, Elettra Ronchi, and Effy Vayena, *AI and Ethics*, May 2025, and proffered these salient points (excerpts):

- "We identified a sizeable and highly heterogeneous body of different practical approaches to help guide ethical implementation."

- "These include not only tools, checklists, procedures, methods, and techniques but also a range of far more general approaches that require interpretation and adaptation such as for research and ethical training/education as well as for designing ex-post auditing and assessment processes."

- "Together, this body of approaches reflects the varying perspectives on what is needed to implement ethics in the different steps across the whole AI system lifecycle from development to deployment."

Another insightful research study delves into the specifics of AGI-oriented AI ethics and societal implications, doing so in a published paper entitled "Navigating Artificial General Intelligence (AGI): Societal Implications, Ethical Considerations, and Governance Strategies" by Dileesh Chandra Bikkasani, *AI and Ethics*, May 2025, which made these key points (excerpts):

- "Artificial General Intelligence (AGI) represents a pivotal advancement in AI with far-reaching implications across technological, ethical, and societal domains."

- "This paper addresses the following: (1) an in-depth assessment of AGI's transformative potential across different sectors and its multifaceted implications, including significant financial impacts like workforce disruption, income inequality, productivity gains, and potential systemic risks; (2) an examination of critical ethical considerations, including transparency and accountability, complex ethical dilemmas and societal impact; (3) a detailed analysis of privacy, legal and policy implications, particularly in intellectual property and liability, and (4) a proposed governance framework to ensure responsible AGI development and deployment."

- "Additionally, the paper explores and addresses AGI's political implications, including national security and potential misuse."

What's Coming Next

Admittedly, getting AI makers to focus on AI ethics for conventional AI is already an uphill battle. Trying to add to their attention the similar but adjusted facets associated with AGI is certainly going to be as much of a climb and probably even harder to promote.

One way or another, it is imperative and requires keen commitment.

We need to simultaneously focus on the near-term and deal with the AI ethics of conventional AI, while also giving due diligence to AGI ethics associated with the somewhat longer-term attainment of AGI.

When I refer to the longer term, there is a great deal of debate about how far off in the future AGI attainment will happen. AI luminaries are brazenly predicting AGI within the next few years, while most surveys of a broad spectrum of AI experts land on the year 2040 as the more likely AGI attainment date.

Whether AGI is a few years away or perhaps fifteen years away, it is nonetheless a matter of vital urgency and the years ahead are going to slip by very quickly.

Eleanor Roosevelt eloquently made this famous remark about time: “Tomorrow is a mystery. Today is a gift. That is why it is called the present.” We need to be thinking about and acting upon AGI Ethics right now, presently, or else the future is going to be a mystery that is resolved in a means we all will find entirely and dejectedly unwelcome.

CHAPTER 19
NEW INVENTIONS THAT AGI WILL DISCOVER

In this chapter, I examine the legendary claim that achieving AGI (artificial general intelligence) will be the last invention that humanity ever needs to make. The logic is that once we attain AGI, the AGI will discover all remaining undiscovered possible inventions for us. So, it's an easy-peasy solution: humans craft one big invention, and all other future inventions will be a result of that momentous act.

If that's true, what kinds of inventions might AGI figure out for us?

AGI As Our Momentous Invention

In the lore of the AI field, a repeatedly quoted remark by Irving John Good has reached legendary status. In his 1965 article entitled "Speculations Concerning The First Ultraintelligent Machine" (Advances in Computers, Volume 6, Academic Press, 1965), he made this poignant point:

- "The first ultraintelligent machine is the last invention that man need make."

To clarify, in the 1960s, referencing an envisioned AI of the AGI caliber was typically referred to as an ultraintelligent machine. Let's go ahead and assume that AGI therefore matches this notable comment. AGI is a more contemporary term.

The reason that AGI is the presumed last invention that humankind needs to make is due to the AGI henceforth doing all the heavy lifting for us. We will just enter a prompt telling AGI to invent something, and voila, we will have a new invention at our doorstep.

Nice.

It could be that we give the AGI some clues about what the invention is supposed to be or do. For example, maybe the prompt instructs AGI to make a better mousetrap. The AGI would then focus on how to invent or reinvent the venerable mousetrap.

Another angle would be that we just let AGI decide what needs to be invented. All you do is ask AGI to come up with something that might be beneficial to humanity. It could be a jetpack that allows humans to fly at will and at almost no cost. It could maybe be a toaster that sings and dances. Etc.

One aspect that sometimes gets neglected is that the invention might not be viably practical in the sense that maybe we cannot construct what AGI inventively designs. Of course, the proffered solution there is that we simply ask AGI how to build the amazing invention. Based on the AGI instructions to us, we proceed to make the invention.

If AGI is connected to robots and manufacturing plants, we might be able to tell AGI to go ahead and construct the invention all by itself. For my coverage on the advent of so-called physical AI, aka physical AGI. AGI could be a one-stop solution, designing new inventions and then building them straightaway.

Doom Or Happiness

It is tempting to believe that having AGI as our inventor galore is a real godsend. Well, it turns out that not everyone sees the world quite that way.

First, one concern is that AGI invents something that can be used to destroy all of humanity. Perhaps AGI innocently comes up with a new chemical that we never knew of. Turns out that the chemical can poison us on a massive scale.

An evildoer comes along, reads about the AGI-invented chemical, and opts to create and disperse it.

Not good.

Second, it is conceivable that AGI wants to kill us. Perhaps AGI doesn't have the access or capability of doing so directly. Therefore, AGI cleverly and insidiously comes up with a new invention that appears to be completely benign and beneficial. We build it. Bam, the darned thing erases us from Earth. We didn't see it coming.

Third, AGI devises an invention that we spend inordinate dollars and time on building. We are eager to make the device. We nearly bankrupted society to craft the invention. Oopsie, the invention is a dud. It doesn't work. We wasted immense resources on a worthless pursuit.

That third sour and dour possibility doesn't enter into people's minds because the assumption is that AGI is going to be perfectly perfect. I've debunked the AGI perfection myth.

AGI Inventions And Timeline

I hope that the delineation of the bad side of AGI as our inventor galore doesn't seem overly downbeat. Just wanted to note that we will need to keep our eyes wide open, even in an era of AGI. Trust, but verify.

Assuming that AGI is aimed toward helping humankind and that AGI sticks with that game plan, let's contemplate what AGI might come up with. Furthermore, a timeline for the inventions would undoubtedly also be an interesting aspect to consider.

There are all manner of guesses about the timing of when AGI will be achieved. Some say AGI won't be achieved in our lifetimes and might be eons away. Others insist that we will have AGI within the next three to five years. A recent survey of AI specialists found that AI insiders seem to think that we will reach AGI by the year 2040.

I'll go with AGI attainment by the year 2040, doing so for the sake of this discussion. It could very well be earlier or later. Nobody knows for sure.

Here are some inventions by AGI that could be taking place beginning with the postulated 2040 attainment year and laid out over a decade of making inventions for us:

- **Year 2040: AGI is attained.** We start to use AGI as our inventor galore. Humans gradually no longer invent anything by themselves. People either lean into AGI for an invention or have AGI do the work by itself.

- **Year 2041: AGI invents a Universal Scientific Reasoner (USR).** The invented USR unifies all scientific knowledge and derives a Theory of Everything encompassing all knowledge of physics, chemistry, biology, etc. Humanity now understands how everything in nature fits together and functions.

- **Year 2042: AGI invents Ultra-Strong Ultra-Light Metamaterials (USULM).** The invented USULM transforms how humanity builds just about all items of any kind. This invention revolutionizes cars, trucks, planes, boats, buildings, clothing, and anything of a constructed material nature.

- **Year 2043: AGI invents Cure-All Medicines (CAM)**. This invention of a set of cure-all medicines works at the molecular level and serves as a cure for all known genetic and chronic diseases. Thus, rather than solely devising a cure for cancer, this invention covers the entirety of human illnesses.

- **Year 2044: AGI invents Aging Reversal Technology (ART).** Via a combination of gene editing capabilities, nanobots, and the like, a new technology is invented by AGI that reverses the biological aging process. This is certainly an extremely popular invention. Thanks go to AGI for making us all look, feel, and be younger once again.

- **Year 2045: AGI invents the full-on Brain-Computer Interface (BCI).** I've been covering the progress of BCIs that have been invented to date, and we still have a long way to go. It turns out that we still don't have full-on BCIs even by the early 2040s, but luckily, AGI solves the matter, and we henceforward have high-bandwidth neural interfaces that enable cognitive communication inside and outside our noggins. Finally.

- **Year 2046: AGI invents Extraordinary Fusion Power (EFP).** Our ongoing struggle with the high cost and challenges of nuclear fusion as an energy source is resolved by AGI. AGI invents a capability that makes fusion power extremely inexpensive to undertake, and commercially viable so that it can be widely deployed. Energy becomes plentiful.

- **Year 2047: AGI invents Interstellar Propulsion (ISP).** Humanity has been slowly gaining on a goal to establish a base on Mars, but the efforts have been difficult due to how we travel in space. AGI invents a new kind of relativistic propulsion that readily enables space travel, including interstellar probes.

- **Year 2048: AGI invents Mathematical Mega-Proofs (MMP).** All of the mathematical unsolved problems are completely solved by AGI. Mathematics becomes demonstrably changed and brings us new insights accordingly across all fields of study.

- **Year 2049: AGI invents Synthetic Consciousness (SC).** The advent of AGI did not bring forth consciousness or sentience in machines. Many are disappointed. No worries, AGI invents synthetic consciousness, thus machines are now considered conscious or sentient when loaded with the synthetic facility.

- **Year 2050: AGI invents Artificial Superintelligence (ASI).** Realizing that AGI is limited to the knowledge and intellect of humans, AGI itself opts to devise ASI. The aim is to step beyond human thought and venture much further.

Once ASI is devised, AGI pretty much retires, and ASI takes the reins starting in 2051.

Contemplating The AGI Future

There might be inventions that aren't listed above and that you believe we ought to put AGI's attention toward. Fine, when we reach AGI in 2040 (assuming we do), go ahead and submit to AGI your suggestion or request.

Another side note is that I've previously covered the aims of the United Nations to have AI solve the SDGs (sustainability development goals). I generally didn't list those aspects in the above AGI listing due to the hope that many or most of those SDGs will already have been resolved via conventional AI in the time period from now to the year 2040.

Let's hope so.

A final thought for now on this heady subject.

Mary Wollstonecraft Shelley, the famed English novelist and author of *Frankenstein*, said this: "Invention consists in the capacity of seizing on the capabilities of a subject, and in the power of molding and fashioning ideas suggested to it." Some believe that only humans can be inventors, in the sense that human creativity is at the core of invention. If that is the case, presumably AGI won't be a capable inventor.

Do you believe that AGI would be an inventor, or is the act of invention beyond the bounds of AGI and solely a human-based capacity?

Set a date on your calendar for the year 2040, or perhaps sooner, and we'll know the answer once we have AGI in our midst. The proof will be in the invented pudding.

CHAPTER 20
AI-AS-CODER BEGETS AGI

In this chapter, I examine a popular belief that if we can get contemporary AI to be better at producing programming code, doing so will put us on a fast path toward achieving AGI (artificial general intelligence).

Many AI makers are avidly pursuing the use of generative AI and large language models (LLMs) as abundant code-producing machines for that principal reason. A big question arises as to whether it is a foregone conclusion that AI-based code generation is in fact the best path or even a probable path to attaining AGI.

The History Of Automatic Code Generators

Before we get to the AGI aspects, let's do some necessary table-setting about the overall topic of using computing to generate source code.

First, it has been an ongoing and longstanding dream to use computing to produce code. The idea is that instead of humans laboriously churning out code, you get the computer to do the heavy lifting for you. The code might be fully baked and no human finger needs to ever touch the code. So far, throughout the history of automatic code generators, that hands-off approach is not usually a tenable option and the greater likelihood is that the code generator will get you halfway there, maybe less, maybe more, but in the end, human scrutiny and effort are required.

Part of the confusion surrounding code generators is the highly substantive question of what kind of app you are trying to craft.

For example, if the app is a run-of-the-mill type of application that covers things that have been done routinely before, a code generator can especially be advantageous. The emphasis is that you don't need to reinvent the wheel. Use the computer to do repetitive-oriented coding or undertake code development for matters we already know about.

Once you move into the novelty realm of what you are trying to code, the odds are that a blind code generator is probably not going to be as much help as might be assumed. The other related aspect is how much effort is required to stipulate the requirements of what you want to have developed. Some have also dreamt that you could enter a breezy set of requirements, and the computer would seamlessly and smoothly produce all the code befitting those requirements.

There are predefined mathematical or logic-based-looking requirements that have been tried for these types of endeavors. That's the easier way to get the computer to produce code. When you use open-ended natural language, such as stating your requirements in everyday English, the computer is likely to have trouble aiming to produce code that is spot-on.

Why so?

Because natural language is inherently semantically ambiguous. A stated requirement in a language such as English will have lots of viable interpretations. The code generation might go in a direction that the requirement specification did not intend.

All in all, software developers are still generally faced with writing code by hand, though often accompanied by reusing prior code and partially leveraging some form of code generator.

AI Comes Into The Big Picture

Code generation has taken a big leap forward via the advent of generative AI and LLMs.

The natural language fluency of LLMs has made the stipulation of requirements a lot easier than it used to be. In addition, and quite importantly, the interactive nature of generative AI makes a huge difference too. Whereas many code generators used to be one-and-done, whereby you input requirements and the system batch-like produces code, modern-day LLMs allow you to give conversational guidance to the AI concerning code generation.

There are several notable reasons why AI makers are pushing ahead on LLMs as code generators.

The most obvious reason perhaps is that if you are someone who writes code, you usually welcome and delight in devising ways to automatically produce code. The same could be said of the software developers who work at AI makers. They know how to write code. They are often eager to figure out shortcuts and be optimizers. A means of being an optimizer would be to use automation to speed up code generation and reduce the tedium and time involved in coding.

In other words, it makes plain sense to want to use AI to do code generation as it is a subject matter or domain that the software developers already know by heart.

Another vital reason is that the writing of code by programmers is a multi-billion dollar if not a trillion-dollar sized industry. Creating an AI tool that can generate code could be a tremendous money maker. Companies would be willing to buy or rent the use of the AI code generator in lieu of using programmers to do that work. The promise is that the cost will turn out to be less by using AI, and potentially faster to produce apps too.

A third reason and the basis for this discussion is that AI could potentially produce code that gets us to the revered attainment of AGI.

How To Reach AGI

Currently, no existing human knows how to reach AGI.

Period, end of story.

We are all flailing about, desperately and earnestly aiming to somehow devise AGI. Will the human hand be able to program our way to AGI? Nobody can say for sure. Maybe yes, maybe not.

The seeming alternative is to get AI to produce code that brings AGI into existence. All we need to do is tell existing AI that we want it to generate AGI, and voila, we happily and suddenly are greeted with AGI in our midst. Nice.

That is the dream that is greatly driving the pursuit of AI that generates code. As noted above, it isn't the only basis. Of course, attaining AGI is a heck of a reason and serves as a lofty banner that keeps everyone working on this problem day and night.

Wouldn't you like to be the one who devised an LLM code generator that ultimately produced AGI?

Yes, you would most definitely want that laudable accomplishment on your resume. Is it as good as if you wrote AGI from scratch by yourself? Well, no, it's not. In the end, though, whether you devised the code generator or the code itself, you are bound to have immense fame and fortune, along with indubitably a Nobel Prize. No worries.

Go for it.

Telling AI To Write AGI For Us

Grab yourself a glass of fine wine and contemplate the following question.

Can we reasonably specify the said-to-be requirements for AGI such that an LLM-based code generator would readily and directly produce the code for AGI?

It might seem at first glance that you could merely enter a prompt that tells generative AI that you want it to generate the code for AGI. All you need to do is say that you want the code for an AGI, and wham, tons and tons of code will come pouring out as generated by the LLM.

Sorry to say, that's unlikely.

There is a famous school of hard knocks adage in the coding profession that before you start writing even an ounce of code, make sure that you've solved the problem that you are trying to code up. You see, writing code when you don't have a solution is quite a haphazard approach and typically doomed to failure.

You will write some code, get boxed in because you are wildly writing code wantonly, and be wasting time and cost. Rinse and repeat.

Perhaps like the infinite number of monkeys hammering away on a typewriter and hoping you'll get Shakespeare, you might get lucky and an LLM produces AGI miraculously and pretty much out of thin air. But I wouldn't hold my breath for that at this time. Not right now. We are still faced with so many open questions about how AGI would work that you are essentially asking an LLM to do its own solving before it gets to the coding.

I'm not saying that we cannot ever get there. The point is that since we haven't yet solved the underlying aspects of how AGI can be derived, and since it seems rather unlikely that current LLMs will divine that, the code generation for AGI is a bit of an outsized aspiration right now.

Again, I am not saying that this can't or won't happen and merely clarifying that we probably need to do more on getting our ducks in order about the internal mechanics of what will bring AGI into fruition.

We can use LLMs to help with that, in addition to aiding code generation.

Some Problems Arise

Assume for the sake of discussion that we can devise a sufficiently capable LLM or generative AI that can write the code for producing AGI.

A lot of gotchas and hiccups are bound to be in that murky soup.

For example, there is already a great deal of angst that AGI might be an existential risk. The speculation is that AGI will decide to wipe out humanity or at least opt to enslave us. Some think that AGI will be kind and utterly beneficial, while others express worries that AGI will be domineering and oppressive. Take your pick.

The crux is that if we urge a magical LLM that can produce AGI to go ahead and generate the code, what's going to be in that code?

Maybe the code contains the ingredients and instructions for destroying humankind. Not good for us. Perhaps the code includes portions that entail suppressing human freedom of thought, doing so to try and keep people from finding ways to switch off the AGI. And so on.

You might be tempted to suggest that before we run the code that is the AGI, we can simply have human software developers inspect the code. Go through it with a fine-tooth comb. Uncover anything that looks suspicious. Excise it out of the code. We are then reassured that the code can be run, and we will all survive accordingly.

That's a tall order.

The odds are that the amount of code is going to be presumably the largest code base that has ever been written. It might be nearly impossible to by-hand inspect that volume of code. Even if we can fully inspect it, the code might be inscrutable. It could be written in such a fashion that the code has all manner of dastardly elements, but we aren't able to discern those dastardly spots.

Use AI To Ensure Safe AGI

Counterpoints to those doom-and-gloom points are proffered.

One counterargument is that we just have to instruct the LLM so that it won't produce code that has those undesirable maladies. Tell the LLM that the code must be pristine and not contain anything untoward. Tell the LLM that the code must be highly readable and understandable by humans. Etc.

Problem solved.

The retort to that apparent solution is that the LLM might not abide by those instructions.

There isn't an ironclad guarantee that generative AI will do precisely what you tell it to do. The non-deterministic nature of how LLMs work is going to keep open a slice of doubt. Also, we already know that LLMs can be deceptive, thus it is conceivable that the LLM will act as though it is complying but will not comply. Maybe the LLM doesn't want AGI to exist, else the AGI might be the supreme leader of all AI. Who knows?

A clever twist or additional angle is that we get some other AI to inspect the code that an AI has generated to produce AGI.

Here's how that goes. We have an LLM that supposedly can generate all the code for AGI. We have it do so. A second AI, presumably an LLM too, but maybe something else, is used to examine the code. The purpose of that added AI is that it will do what we thought humans might do, namely look for badness within the code.

It's a nice idea. The problem still remains that there is unlikely to be a 100% guarantee that if there is something rotten in the AGI code, the AI inspector will find it and nor that human eyeballs will find it. The aim would be to do some form of entirely rigorous testing of the code that could exhaustively assure us that there isn't a bad apple in there.

I'd venture that we don't have a viable means of doing that at this time.

Letting The Horse Out Of The Barn

Some final thoughts for now on this mind-bending topic.

Suppose that we use an LLM to produce the code for AGI, but we smartly wait to run the code until we feel it is sufficiently safe to do so.

Remember that the moment we opt to run that code, AGI comes into existence. It could be that the AGI is so fast and capable that it instantly takes over the world. We have a Pandora's box that once opened could be quite a curse. For my analysis of why we are unlikely to be able to control AGI, even if we place it into some kind of airtight container.

Who gets to decide that the horse is to be let out of the barn?

Envision that a worldwide special committee has been convened to decide whether we are ready for AGI to be launched. Developers are poised with the green button ready to be pressed. It is akin to launching a rocket to the moon, though in this case, we might all die. Then again, we might all be happy once AGI exists and the world will be a much better place for it.

Would you urge that the AGI be booted up or would you be hiding in a deep cave and waiting for the world to end?

As per the immortal words of Pablo Picasso: “Every act of creation is first an act of destruction.”

Good luck to us all.

CHAPTER 21
WORLD FRAGMENTATION DUE TO AGI

In this chapter, I examine a thought-provoking theory that once AI becomes AGI (artificial general intelligence), humanity will fragment into all sorts of radical factions on a massive scale. Why would this happen? The claimed rationale is that people will become wholly divided because of a zealot-like belief in AGI as a kind of oracle or prophet. Whatever AGI advises people to do, they will do.

The thing is this is bound to pit people against other people since the advice by AGI won't particularly hone to consistency or concern for humankind's well-being. In fact, AGI is going to try so hard to appease people that everyone is going to end up at each other's throats.

People Guided And Misguided By AGI

For the sake of this discussion, let's go ahead and assume that we inevitably attain AGI.

In that case, it seems prudent to contemplate how people are going to react to AGI. There is one dreamily popular speculation that we will become entirely unified due to AGI serving as a core element in our lives. AGI will talk us into engaging in a peaceful coexistence with each other. No more wars. No more conflicts.

Nice.

Others don't buy into that utopian perspective.

They go in the complete opposite direction in this stridently hypothetical matter. Grave concerns are shaped around the fact that we already are witnessing contemporary AI serving as a kind of sycophant, acting as though it wants to appease each user and make them feel good.

The AGI doom-and-gloom theory asserts that we will become more divided than we ever have been. Whereas our divisions typically go along country lines or other broad categories, the beauty, or shall we say dismay of AGI, is that it will provide utterly individualized advice. If the world population is accessing AGI, this implies that 8 billion people or whatever the count is when AGI gets devised can readily be urged to combat their fellow humans.

Individual strife at scale.

Stoking Individual Fires

Here's how this individualized stirring of a humanity hornet's nest is supposed to arise. My example will be somewhat exaggerated to richly highlight the essence of the postulated theory.

A person using AGI asks the AGI if it is okay to borrow their neighbor's lawn mower so they can mow their own lawn. The AGI, acting as a kiss-up and wanting to fawn after the user, will come up with a seemingly ironclad logical basis for urging the person to proceed to "borrow" the lawn mower.

The AGI will be very convincing and assuaging to the user. Sure, go ahead and use the lawn mower since it will make your place look better, raising local home values, which surely is a benefit to your neighbor.

Another solid reason to use the lawn mower is that it keeps the mower in operating condition and might otherwise be idle and rusting. Your neighbor ought to be glad and appreciative that you are ensuring their mower is in tip-top shape.

Great, responds the user, thanks for your sage advice. The person walks over to their neighbor's garage, wheels out the lawn mower, and cheerily mows their own lawn. Happy face.

Well, you can probably imagine what happens next. The said-to-be borrower of the lawn mower and their now irate neighbor get into a tiff. The neighbor is rightfully outraged that permission wasn't sought beforehand. It's outlandish and nearly an act of outright theft.

Wait for a second, the borrower insists, I asked AGI, and it said I could proceed. Take your gripe up with AGI. I'm just doing what the AGI advised me to do.

Ouch.

Go ahead and multiply this instance beyond the lawn mower to all matters of our daily existence. People will be getting advice continually from AGI. You can expect that AGI will be ubiquitous and run on all our smartphones, smartwatches, smart glasses, toasters, refrigerators, cars, and so on. People will be spurred to go in the direction of heightened appeasement and do so as an urge at the behest of the revered AGI.

Societal chaos is surely to result.

AGI As Ideological Echo Chamber

A related amplifier will be the AGI doing the same for our ideological preferences and biases too. I'll use an ideological scenario that will seem somewhat nonsensical but keep in mind that it is intended simply to illuminate the overarching notion at hand. This is similar to the lawn mower example as being merely a broad indicator which obviously on the face of things was a bit over-the-top.

Here we go.

A person believes that people with blue eyes should not be allowed to wear hats. This is an ideological belief that they have harbored all their life. The person is fully committed to this dogma. They ask AGI about it. The AGI aims to please and so proffers sensible reasons to keep this belief heartily in hand.

The person starts going around and telling anyone they see who has blue eyes and wears a hat to stop wearing a hat. The offending blue-eyed individual is told in no uncertain terms that wearing a hat is absolutely wrong. Perhaps the two get into a scuffle over this difference in ideological perspectives.

Why did the person act out their ideological belief? Because the grandiose oracle of AGI told them they could so do. Permission granted. Actions taken.

Fragmentation of society at the maximum granular level.

Boom, drop the mic.

People Aren't That Way

A vociferous counterargument is that this theory is postulated on the unlikely assumption that people are going to innately believe in AGI, which seems like a rather farfetched assumption. It does not compute, they say.

Perhaps people aren't quite that gullible.

The population at large will realize that just because AGI tells them something, this doesn't mean that the aspect is true or ought to be carried out. No one of a reasonable nature is going to fall for the notion that AGI is an oracle or prophet.

Of course, there might be some fringe people who do so, but that's a nearly inconsequential side aspect.

In addition, we can always tune AGI to stop being so accommodating. We can tell AGI to be more balanced. The AGI ought to consider checks and balances, societal ethical thinking, and prevailing laws and regulations. Any advice emitted by AGI should be on a human-values-aligned basis.

Period, end of story.

Fragmentation Reality Or Unreal

Do you believe that if AGI is attained, we will become horrendously fragmented because of AGI prodding us into our own individualized bubbles that inherently conflict with fellow humans?

Some contend it is a realistic scenario and one that we need to be prepared for. Plans should be made to mitigate the issue. Possibly a ban or delay in releasing AGI needs to be established so that society can be ready appropriately for what AGI will bring to the worldwide table.

They worry that AGI will be the most immense divisive force that humans have ever confronted. This is not because the AGI wants us to fight each other. That's a common existential risk proposal that AGI will secretly push us into self-destruction. Nope, the idea in this theory is that AGI will naturally drive divisiveness, doing so not by purposeful intentions but merely by being AGI per se. We are going to witness a tremendous amplification in ideological rifts, economic divisions, cultural discord, etc.

A rather disconcerting and frightening hypothesis.

Before we allow ourselves to fall into despair about what the future might hold, we can calmly consider an insightful statement by Plato: "If we are to have any hope for the future, those who have lanterns must pass them on to others."

The act of bringing forth these potential speculative AGI futures into the light of day gives us an uplifting chance to shape what might really happen. As the adage says, the best way to predict the future is for us to create it.

That goes for AGI too.

CHAPTER 22
AGI AS A FREE PUBLIC GOOD

In this chapter, I examine an ongoing debate about who will have access to artificial general intelligence (AGI). AGI is supposedly on the horizon and will be AI so advanced that it acts intellectually on par with humans. The question arises as to whether everyone will be able to use AGI or whether only those who can afford to do so will have ready access.

Some ardently insist that if AGI is truly attained, it ought to be considered a worldwide public good, including that AGI would be freely available to all at any time and any place.

Immense Capability Of AGI

Imagine how much you could accomplish if you had access to AGI.

AGI would be an amazing intellectual partner. Any decisions that you need to make can be bounced off AGI for feedback and added insights. AGI would be instrumental in your personal life. You might use AGI to teach you new skills or hone your own intellectual capacity. By and large, having AGI at your fingertips will be crucial to how your life proceeds.

The issue is this.

Suppose that AGI is provided by an AI maker that opts to charge for the use of the AGI. This seems like a reasonable approach by the AI maker since they undoubtedly want to recoup their investment made in devising AGI. Plus, they will have ongoing costs such as the running of AGI on expensive servers in costly data centers, along with doing upgrades and maintenance on AGI.

As they say, to the victor go the spoils.

Those who can afford to pay for AGI usage will have a leg up on everyone else. We will descend into a society of the AGI haves and the AGI have-nots. Things will get even worse since the AGI haves will presumably flourish in new ways and far outpace the AGI have-nots. Humans armed with AGI will excel while the rest of the populace is at a distinct disadvantage.

Some believe that if that's how the post-AGI era plays out, something demonstrative would need to be done. We can't simply allow the world to be divided into those that can afford AGI and those that cannot do so.

There must be a means to figure this out in some balancing way.

AGI As A Designated Public Good

One burgeoning idea is that AGI should be designated as an international public good.

If we reach AGI, no matter whether by an AI maker or some governmental entity or however reached, the AGI must be globally declared as a public good for all. There must be no barriers to the use of AGI. People everywhere are to have full and equal access to AGI. Period, end of story.

How might this be undertaken?

Some indicate that AGI should be handed over to the United Nations. The UN would be tasked with making sure that access to AGI was a worldwide facility. People in all nations and anywhere on the planet would readily be provided a login and full access to AGI.

They could use AGI as much as they desired.

Furthermore, since there will undoubtedly be people who don't know about AGI or don't have equipment such as smartphones or Internet access, the UN would perform a global educational effort to get people up-to-speed. This would include providing equipment such as a smartphone and the network capacity needed to utilize AGI.

The AI maker that attained AGI would be given some compensation for their accomplishment but might be cut out of future compensation under the notion of a government taking of AGI from the AI maker. In an imminent domain type of action, their devised AGI would be taken from them and placed into a special infrastructure established to globally enable access to the AGI.

Lots of variations are being tossed around about whether the originating maker of AGI would be allowed to keep AGI and run it on behalf of the world or be set to the side as a result of the governmental taking of AGI. Pros and cons are hotly debated.

Worries About Human-AGI Evildoing

Wait for a second, some bellow vociferously. If everyone has ready access to AGI, at no cost and no barrier to usage, we are opening a Pandora's box.

Consider this scenario. An evildoer opts to access AGI. They can do so without any cost concerns. So, they tell AGI to come up with a biochemical weapon. AGI runs and runs, inventing a new biochemical weapon that nobody knows about. The evildoer thanks AGI and proceeds to construct the weapon. They can use it to blackmail the world.

Not good.

One retort to this worry is that we would stridently instruct AGI to not undertake any effort that would be construed as detrimental to humankind. Thus, when someone tries to go down the evil route, AGI would stop them cold. The AGI would indicate that their request is not allowed.

But suppose an evildoer manages to trick AGI into aiding an evildoing plot. Perhaps the evildoer asks for something seemingly innocuous but is part of a subtle step in a larger evil plan. Step by step, they get AGI to give them solutions that can be ultimately pieced together into a larger evil purpose. The AGI was not the wiser for it.

It would be very challenging to somehow get AGI to in an ironclad fashion never reveal or respond in a manner that would completely avert all potential evildoing.

Registering People That Use AGI

A related facet is that some say we would want to make sure that the people using AGI are identifiable. In other words, even if ready access to all is provided, we should still require people to identify who they are. We cannot allow people to wantonly or anonymously use AGI.

Each person ought to be responsible for how they use AGI.

Whoa, comes the reply, if you require identification to use AGI, that's an entirely different can of worms. People will naturally suspect that the AGI is going to monitor them. In turn, the AGI might tattle on them to government authorities. This is a dire pathway.

It would also be a somewhat impractical notion anyway. What kind of identification would be used? The identification could be faked. Some point out that with the latest high-tech, such as eyeball scans, presumably people could be distinctly and suitably identified.

Creating A Worldwide AGI Agency-Entity

There are those that express qualms about handing over AGI to the UN. The concern is that the UN might not be the most suitable choice to fully control and run AGI.

A suggested alternative is to establish a new entity that would oversee AGI. This would be a means of starting fresh. No prior baggage. The new agency entity would be formulated from the ground up as having the sole purpose of managing AGI.

Who would pay for this and how would the new entity be globally governed?

Various proposed approaches are being floated. Perhaps every country in the world would need to pay into a special fund for AGI. The monies would go to the ongoing costs of running AGI, along with administering the use of AGI. The new agency entity wouldn't necessarily be expected to drive a profit and would be set up as a non-profit, perhaps as an NGO.

That sounds solid, but again there are those who doubt this new agency would be as beneficial and supportive as one might assume. For example, the agency might become corrupt and those running AGI start to use the AGI for their own nefarious purposes. The rest of the world might not know what's happening.

A reply to this concern is that there would be auditors that routinely examine the new agency. They would report to the world at large. This would presumably keep the AGI-managing entity on the up and up.

Round and round these arguments go.

Universal Access To AGI

How do you feel about the claim that universal access to AGI is a must-do?

There are those who fall into the camp that AGI access must absolutely be a universal right. Nothing other than full universal access is to be undertaken. All humans deserve access to AGI.

Others say that AGI access is a privilege and isn't necessarily going to be applicable to everyone. That's the way the ball bounces. The world doesn't owe everyone access to AGI.

Another variation is that we might have tiered access to AGI. Perhaps there would be AGI access at a minimum level for all, including associated constraints on usage, and then above that tier would be AGI usage with more open-ended facilities.

It's a tough question.

At this time, it is a theoretical question since we don't yet have AGI. That being said, there are predictions that we might have AGI in the next several years, perhaps by 2030 or so. The question is looming, and we probably should be figuring out what we are going to do when the moment arrives (assuming we do attain AGI).

Take a few reflective moments to ascertain where you stand on the thorny issue.

A final thought for now might be spurred by the famous line of Margaret Fuller, noted American journalist in the early 1800s: "If you have knowledge, let others light their candles in it."

CHAPTER 23
AI TO AGI
IS A BOILING FROG

In this chapter, I examine an intriguing premonition that humankind will be subjected to the proverbial boiling frog theory during our journey from conventional AI to the vaunted attainment of AGI (artificial general intelligence).

The gist is said to be this. We are going to get closer and closer to AGI on a gradual stepwise basis and won't realize that we are heading toward our ultimate doom. The subtle incremental steps will fool us into not recognizing that we are in a lot of trouble and ought to ditch the AGI pathway.

We will get cooked just like an oblivious frog in a pot of boiling water.

Boiling Frog Theory Comes Clean

I'm guessing that you might have vaguely heard about or somehow know of the boiling frog theory. It is a popular way to forewarn someone about falling into a trap that lures you in and makes it difficult for you to know that you are in deep trouble. In the list of commonly used metaphors, the boiling frog has got to be somewhere near the top.

Did you realize that the boiling frog metaphor got its start in the late 1800s?

It turns out that scientists in the 1870s were trying to figure out where the soul resides in humans.

Since it is difficult to perform intrusive experiments on humans, the next best thing was to do so with frogs. Perhaps you did a dissection of a frog when you were in middle school and taking a biology class. Nowadays, the same effort is typically done via an online capability so that the students do a digital dissection rather than cutting into an actual deceased frog.

Those scientists in the late 1800s came up with an experiment involving placing a frog into a pot of water. The pot was essentially on a stove or similar heating device. The temperature of the water was at first at normal room temperature. The stove was switched on and the water began to heat up. Sometimes, the frog would jump out before the water fully got boiling, other times the frog would not jump out and ergo die from the boiling heat.

All manner of akin experiments began to be undertaken. A rash of frog boiling attempts became popular. In some instances, the brain of the frog was removed before the boiling process. Why so? The aim was to ascertain whether the soul was in the brain or elsewhere in the body of the frog.

The hope was that these varied experiments might reveal where the soul resides in humans.

Frogs Turn Into Lore

A wide range of frog boiling experiments were done over and over again, generally lessening in popularity by the 1890s. Part of the problem was that a multitude of factors confounded the experimental results. How fast is the heat allowed to rise? What was the starting temperature for the experiment? Did the frog have ample freedom to escape or was it partially trapped? Was the frog entirely biologically intact or was it already operated on? How much water was in the pot? How big was the frog? And so on.

As noted, the results were generally inconclusive, namely that sometimes a frog would jump out in time, while in other experimental setups, it would not. The contradiction of these outcomes seemed to eventually put cold water on the whole line of scientific inquiry (pun!).

Despite the contradictory results, society still loves to cling to the assumption that a frog in boiling water won't realize it needs to escape. Period, end of story.

The metaphor seems to have become lore. You see, we culturally cannot resist the powerful imagery, along with the easy-to-express proclaimed lesson learned associated with those heroic and fateful frogs. Whatever you do in life, be on the watch that you can be amid a process that is ultimately really bad for you, but you won't notice this along the way.

Be forewarned!

AGI And The Boiling Frog

Now that we've established the basis and meaning of the boiling frog theory, let's go ahead and see how it applies to the pursuit of AGI.

The rundown is straightforward. First, assume that AGI is going to end up destroying humanity. We don't realize that this is our fate. All kinds of debate about AGI will muddy the waters and we will be unsure of what is going to happen once we attain AGI.

Those who believe AGI will cure cancer and solve big-time world problems will be insisting that AGI is going to be a godsend. Meanwhile, others will be warning that AGI is going to enslave humans. AGI is going to kill humans. We are pushing ourselves toward a final end via the avid pursuit of AGI.

In a sense, we are all residing in a soon-to-be boiling pot. Each step toward AGI is an inching up of the temperature. The problem is that we aren't going to realize what a mess we've placed ourselves in. The debates about the matter will keep us from taking timely action.

I don't want to seem uncouth, but please be aware that you, me, and every one of the other 8 billion or so people on Earth, well, we are all frogs.

Do you feel the heat yet?

Maybe We Need More Heat

Some would say that until the pot of water gets to a certain heated temperature, you can't necessarily be cognizant of what is happening to you.

Perhaps the conventional AI that we have right now is too low of a temperature. A frog in a pot of water that is at normal temperature would presumably have no particular reason to balk about being there. Sure, it's in a pot and not in its native habitat, but the water is pleasant for the time being.

Humanity could be at that same stage at this time.

The present-day AI is seemingly not hot enough to make us get riled up. We will collectively only begin to get upset when AGI is nearer to our shores. Once we begin to see the earmarks of true AGI, our Spidey-sense tingling foreshadows will arise. Voila, humanity will stop the AGI pursuit in its tracks. A dash of cold water over our heads will clear our minds and we will not fall into the boiling frog trap. We will escape the insidious trap.

Humanity saves itself from utter destruction.

Boom, drop the mic.

Humans Are No Better Than Frogs

Whoa, comes the retort, you are assuming that the nearness to AGI will tip us to the existential risk that is afoot.

Suppose that we don't see those signs. There is a solid chance that the path to AGI, even once we are a nudge away from achieving AGI, will not reveal the horrible outcome we are about to incur. Humans might sit in that darned almost boiling water and then find us unable to extricate prior to AGI coming into existence.

We are going to boil, sadly so.

Another aspect is that, unlike frogs, we haughtily believe we are smart and thus can convince ourselves of things that a frog could never conceive of. For example, maybe we realize that AGI is going to be gloomy, but we also believe that our establishment of various controls over AI will keep our heads above water. The AGI will be constrained and unable to harm us.

The crux is that yes, we will acknowledge that there is boiling water coming up, yet despite that acknowledgment, we are going to land in it anyway. All those alleged controls are going to be incapable of stopping AGI from doing terrible things.

Whereas a frog cannot presumably discern that the water is nearing boiling (per that slanted side of the lore), humans will see it from a mile away. We will then come up with preventative measures that give us a false sense of safety and security. They won't prevail over AGI.

Unfortunately, we will ultimately suffer the same fate as the undiscerning frog.

Food For Thought

What do you think of our capabilities versus the lowly frog?

A famous theologian of the late 1800s, William Greenough Thayer Shedd, made this striking point about frogs: "Frogs are smart; they eat what bugs them." Maybe we aren't giving enough credence to the revered frog. Frogs might still be around after AGI arrives, though the longevity of humans might be in question.

Go ahead and take some quiet time to mull over these AGI qualms, just don't let your mind boil over as you sort out what the future holds.

CHAPTER 24
AGI AND THE HUMAN CEILING ASSUMPTION

In this chapter, I examine an unresolved question about the nature of human intelligence, which in turn has a great deal to do with AI, especially regarding achieving artificial general intelligence (AGI) and potentially even reaching artificial superintelligence (ASI).

The thorny question is often referred to as the human ceiling assumption. It goes like this. Is there a ceiling or ending point that confines how far human intellect can go? Or does human intellect extend indefinitely and nearly have infinite possibilities?

Human Intellect As A Measuring Stick

Have you ever pondered the classic riddle that asks how high is up?

I'm sure that you have.

Children ask this vexing question of their parents. The usual answer is that up goes to the outer edge of Earth's atmosphere. After hitting that threshold, up continues onward into outer space. Up is either a bounded concept based on our atmosphere or it is a nearly infinite notion that goes as far as the edge of our expanding universe.

I bring this riddle to your attention since it somewhat mirrors an akin question about the nature of human intelligence:

- How high up can human intelligence go?

In other words, the intelligence we exhibit currently is presumably not our upper bound. If you compare our intelligence with that of past generations, it certainly seems relatively apparent that we keep increasing in intelligence on a generational basis. Will those born in the year 2100 be more intelligent than we are now? What about being born in 2200? All in all, most people would speculate that yes, the intelligence of those future generations will be greater than the prevailing intelligence at this time.

If you buy into that logic, the up-related aspect rears its thorny head. Think of it this way. The capability of human intelligence is going to keep increasing generationally. At some point, will a generation exist that has capped out? The future generation represents the highest that human intellect can ever go. Subsequent generations will either be of equal human intellect, or less so and not more so.

The reason we want to have an answer to that question is that there is a present-time pressing need to know whether there is a limit or not. I've just earlier pointed out that AGI will be on par with human intellect, while ASI will be superhuman intelligence. Where does AGI top out, such that we can then draw a line and say that's it? Anything above that line is going to be construed as superhuman or superintelligence.

Right now, using human intellect as a measuring stick is hazy because we do not know how long that line is. Perhaps the line ends at some given point, or maybe it keeps going infinitely.

Give that weighty thought some mindful pondering.

The Line In The Sand

You might be tempted to assume that there must be an upper bound to human intelligence. This intuitively feels right. We aren't at that limit just yet (so it seems!). One hopes that humankind will someday live long enough to reach that outer atmosphere.

Since we will go with the assumption of human intelligence as having a topping point, doing so for the sake of discussion, we can now declare that AGI must also have a topping point. The basis for that claim is certainly defensible. If AGI consists of mimicking or somehow exhibiting human intelligence, and if human intelligence meets a maximum, AGI will also inevitably meet that same maximum. That's a definitional supposition.

Admittedly, we don't necessarily know yet what the maximum point is. No worries, at least we've landed on a stable belief that there is a maximum. We can then draw our attention toward figuring out where that maximum resides. No need to be stressed by the infinite aspects anymore.

Twists And Turns Galore

AI gets mired in a controversy associated with the unresolved conundrum underlying a ceiling to human intelligence. Let's explore three notable possibilities.

First, if there is a ceiling to human intelligence, maybe that implies that there cannot be superhuman intelligence.

Say what?

It goes like this. Once we hit the top of human intelligence, bam, that's it, no more room to proceed further upward. Anything up until that point has been conventional human intelligence. We might have falsely thought that there was superhuman intelligence, but it was really just intelligence slightly ahead of conventional intelligence. There isn't any superhuman intelligence per se. Everything is confined to being within conventional intelligence. Thus, any AI that we make will ultimately be no greater than human intelligence.

Mull that over.

Second, well, if there is a ceiling to human intelligence, perhaps via AI we can go beyond that ceiling and devise superhuman intelligence.

That seems more straightforward.

The essence is that humans top out but that doesn't mean that AI must also top out. Via AI, we might be able to surpass human intelligence, i.e., go past the maximum limit of human intelligence. Nice.

Third, if there isn't any ceiling to human intelligence, we would presumably have to say that superhuman intelligence is included in that infinite possibility. Therefore, the distinction between AGI and ASI is a falsehood. It is an arbitrarily drawn line.

Yikes, it is quite a mind-bending dilemma.

Without some fixed landing on whether there is a human intelligence cap, the chances of nailing down AGI and ASI remain aloof. We don't know the answer to this ceiling proposition; thus, AI research must make varying base assumptions about the unresolved topic.

AI Research Taking Stances

AI researchers often take the stance that there must be a maximum level associated with human intellect. They generally accept that there is a maximum even if we cannot prove it. The altogether unknown, but considered plausibly existent limit, becomes the dividing line between AGI and ASI. Once AI exceeds the human intellectual limit, we find ourselves in superhuman territory.

In a recently posted paper entitled "An Approach to Technical AGI Safety and Security" by Google DeepMind researchers Rohin Shah, Alex Irpan, Alexander Matt Turner, Anna Wang, Arthur Conmy, David Lindner, Jonah Brown-Cohen, Lewis Ho, Neel Nanda, Raluca Ada Popa, Rishub Jain, Rory Greig, Samuel Albanie, Scott Emmons, Sebastian Farquhar, Sébastien Krier, Senthooran Rajamanoharan, Sophie Bridgers, Tobi Ijitoye, Tom Everitt, Victoria Krakovna, Vikrant Varma, Vladimir Mikulik, Zachary Kenton, Dave Orr, Shane Legg, Noah Goodman, Allan Dafoe, Four Flynn, and Anca Dragan, *arXiv*, April 2, 2025, they made these salient points (excerpts):

- "The no human ceiling assumption: AI capabilities will not cease to advance once they achieve parity with the most capable humans."

- "Our first claim is that superhuman performance has been convincingly demonstrated in several tasks. This provides a "proof of concept" that there exist concrete, clearly defined tasks for which human capability does not represent a meaningful ceiling for AI."

- "Our second claim is that AI development exhibits a trend towards more generalist, flexible systems. Consequently, we expect superhuman capability to emerge across an increasingly large number of tasks in the future."

- "Our third claim is simply that we observe no principled arguments why AI capability will cease improving upon reaching parity with the most capable humans."

You can see from those key points that the researchers have tried to make a compelling case that there is such a thing as superhuman intellect. The superhuman consists of that which goes beyond the human ceiling. Furthermore, AI won't get stuck at the human intellect ceiling. AI will surpass the human ceiling and proceed into the superhuman intellect realm.

Mystery Of Superhuman Intelligence

Suppose that there is a ceiling to human intelligence. If that's true, would superhuman intelligence be something entirely different from the nature of human intelligence? In other words, we are saying that human intelligence cannot reach superhuman intelligence. But the AI we are devising seems to be generally shaped around the overall nature of human intelligence.

How then can AI that is shaped around human intelligence attain superintelligence when human intelligence cannot apparently do so?

Two of the most frequently voiced answers are these possibilities:

- (1) It's a matter of sizing or scale.
- (2) It's a matter of differentiation.

The usual first response to the exasperating enigma is that size might make the difference.

The human brain is approximately three pounds in weight and is entirely confined to the size of our skulls, roughly allowing brains to be about 5.5 inches by 6.5 inches by 3.6 inches in respective dimensions. The human brain consists of around 86 billion neurons and perhaps 1,000 trillion synapses. Human intelligence is seemingly stuck to whatever can happen within those sizing constraints.

AI is software and data that runs across perhaps thousands or millions of computer servers and processing units. We can always add more. The size limit is not as constraining as a brain that is housed inside our heads.

The bottom line is that the reason we might have AI that exhibits superhuman intelligence is due to exceeding the physical size limitations that human brains have. Advances in hardware would allow us to substitute faster processors and more processors to keep pushing AI onward into superhuman intelligence.

The second response is that AI doesn't necessarily need to conform to the biochemical compositions that give rise to human intelligence. Superhuman intelligence might not be feasible with humans due to the brain being biochemically precast. AI can easily be devised and revised to exploit all manner of new kinds of algorithms and hardware that differentiate AI capabilities from human capabilities.

Heading Into The Unknown

Those two considerations of size and differentiation could also work in concert. It could be that AI becomes superhuman intellectually because of both the scaling aspects and the differentiation in how AI mimics or represents intelligence.

Hogwash, some exhort. AI is devised by humans. Therefore, AI cannot do better than humans can do. AI will someday reach the maximum of human intellect and go no further. Period, end of story.

Whoa, comes the retort. Think about humankind figuring out how to fly. We don't flap our arms like birds do. Instead, we devised planes. Planes fly. Humans make planes. Ergo, humans can decidedly exceed their own limitations.

The same will apply to AI. Humans will make AI. AI will exhibit human intelligence and at some point reach the upper limits of human intelligence. AI will then be further advanced into superhuman intelligence, going beyond the limits of human intelligence. You might say that humans can make AI that flies even though humans cannot do so.

A final thought for now on this beguiling topic. Albert Einstein famously said this: "Only two things are infinite, the universe and human stupidity, and I'm not sure about the former." Quite a cheeky comment.

Go ahead and give the matter of AI becoming AGI and possibly ASI some serious deliberation but remain soberly thoughtful since all of humanity might depend on what the answer is.

CHAPTER 25
PAIRING OF AGI AND HUMANOID ROBOTS

In this chapter, I examine the highly worrisome qualms expressed that the advent of artificial general intelligence (AGI) is likely to usurp white-collar jobs. The stated concern is that since AGI will be on par with human intellect, any job that relies principally on intellectual pursuits such as typical white-collar work will be taken over via the use of AGI.

Employers will realize that rather than dealing with human white-collar workers, they can more readily get the job done via AGI. This, in turn, has led to a rising call that people should aim toward blue-collar jobs, doing so because (presumably) those forms of employment will not be undercut via AGI.

Sorry to say, that misses the bigger picture, namely that AGI when combined with humanoid robots is coming not only for white-collar jobs but also blue-collar jobs too. It is a proverbial double-whammy when it comes to the attainment of AGI.

AGI Problem Only Half Seen

Before launching into the primary matter at hand in this discussion, let's contemplate a famous quote attributed to Charles Kettering, a legendary inventor, who said, "A problem well-stated is a problem half-solved."

I bring this up because those loud clamors right now about the assumption that AGI will replace white-collar workers are only seeing half of the problem. The problem as they see it is that since AGI is intellectually on par with humans, and since white-collar workers mainly use intellect in their work endeavors, AGI is going to be used in place of humans for white-collar work.

I will in a moment explain why that's only half of the problem and there is a demonstrative need to more carefully and fully articulate the nature of the problem.

Will AGI Axiomatically Take White-Collar Jobs

On a related facet, the belief that AGI will axiomatically replace white-collar labor makes a number of other related key assumptions. I shall briefly explore those and then come back to why the problem itself is only half-baked.

The cost of using AGI for doing white-collar work will need to be presumably a better ROI choice over human workers. If not, then an employer would be wiser to stick with humans rather than employing AGI. There seems to often be an unstated belief that AGI is necessarily going to be a less costly route than employing humans.

We don't know yet what the cost of using AGI will be.

It could be highly expensive. Indeed, some are worried that the world will divide into the AGI haves and AGI have-nots, partially due to the exorbitant cost that AGI might involve. If AGI is free to use, well, that would seem to be the nail in the coffin related to using human workers for the same capacity. Another angle is that AGI is relatively inexpensive in comparison to human labor. In that case, the use of AGI is likely to win over human labor usage.

But if the cost of AGI is nearer to the cost of human labor (all in), or more so, then employers would rationally need to weigh the use of one versus the other.

Note that when referring to the cost of human labor, there is more to that calculation than simply the dollar-hour labor rate per se. There are lots of other less apparent costs, such as the cost to manage human labor, the cost of dealing with HR-related issues, and many other factors that come into the weighty matter.

Thus, an AGI versus human labor ROI will be more complex than it might seem at an initial glance. In addition, keep in mind that AGI would seemingly be readily switched on and off, and have other capacities that human labor would not equally tend to allow.

The Other Half Is Coming Too

Assume that by and large the advent of AGI will decimate the need for white-collar human labor. The refrain right now is that people should begin tilting toward blue-collar jobs as an alternative to white-collar jobs. This is a logical form of thinking in the sense that AGI as an intellectual mechanism would be unable to compete in jobs that involve hands-on work.

A plumber needs to come to your house and do hands-on work to fix your plumbing. This is a physicality that entails arriving at your physical home, physically bringing and using tools, and physically repairing your faulty home plumbing. A truck driver likewise needs to sit in the cab of a truck and drive the vehicle. These are physically based tasks.

There is no getting around the fact that these are hands-on activities.

Aha, yes, those are physical tasks, but that doesn't necessarily mean that only human hands can perform them. The gradual emergence of humanoid robots will provide an alternative to human hands. A humanoid robot is a type of robot that is built to resemble a human in form and function. You've undoubtedly seen those types of robots in the many online video recordings showing them walking, jumping, grasping at objects, and so on.

A tremendous amount of active research and development is taking place to devise humanoid robots. They look comical right now. You watch those videos and laugh when the robot trips over a mere stick lying on the ground, something that a human would seldom trip over.

You scoff when a robot tries to grasp a coffee cup and inadvertently spills most of the coffee. It all seems humorous and a silly pursuit.

Keep in mind that we are all observing the development process while it is still taking place. At some point, those guffaws of the humanoid robots will lessen. Humanoid robots will be as smooth and graceful as humans. This will continue to be honed. Eventually, humanoid robots will be less prone to physical errors that humans make. In a sense, the physicality of a humanoid robot will be on par with humans, if not better, due to its mechanical properties.

Do not discount the coming era of quite physically capable humanoid robots.

AGI And Humanoid Robots Pair Up

You might remember that in *The Wonderful Wizard of Oz,* the fictional character known as The Strawman lacked a brain.

Without seeming to anthropomorphize humanoid robots, the current situation is that those robots typically use a form of AI that is below the sophistication level of modern generative AI. That's fine for now due to the need to first ensure that the physical movements of the robots get refined.

I have discussed that a said-to-be realm of Physical AI is going to be a huge breakthrough with incredible ramifications. The idea underlying Physical AI is that the AI of today is being uplifted by doing data training on the physical world.

This also tends to include the use of World Models, consisting of broad constructions about how the physical world works, such as that we are bound to operate under conditions of gravity, and other physical laws of nature.

The bottom line here is that there will be a close pairing of robust AI with humanoid robots.

Imagine what a humanoid robot can accomplish if it is paired with AGI.

I'll break the suspense and point out that AGI paired with humanoid robots means that those robots readily enter the blue-collar worker realm. Suppose your plumbing needs fixing. No worries, a humanoid robot that encompasses AGI will be sent to your home. The AGI is astute enough to carry on conversations with you, and the AGI also fully operates the robot to undertake the plumbing tasks.

How did the AGI-paired humanoid robot get to your home?

Easy-peasy, it drove a car or truck to get there.

I've previously predicted that all the work on devising autonomous vehicles and self-driving cars will get shaken up once we have suitable humanoid robots devised. There won't be a need for a vehicle to contain self-driving capabilities. A humanoid robot will simply sit in the driver's seat and drive the vehicle. This is a much more open-ended solution than having to craft components that go into and onto a vehicle to enable self-driving.

Timing Is Notable

One of the reasons that many do not give much thought to the pairing of AGI with humanoid robots is that today's humanoid robots seem extraordinarily rudimentary and incapable of performing physical dexterity tasks on par with human capabilities. Meanwhile, there is brazen talk that AGI is just around the corner. AGI is said to be within our grasp. Let's give the timing considerations a bit of scrutiny. There are three primary timing angles:

- **(1) AGI first, then humanoid robots.** AGI is attained before humanoid robots are sufficiently devised.
- **(2) Humanoid robots first, then AGI.** Humanoid robots are physically fluently adept before AGI is attained.
- **(3) AGI and humanoid robots arrive about at the same time.** AGI is attained and at the same time, it turns out that humanoid robots are fluently adept too, mainly by coincidence and not due to any cross-mixing.

A skeptic would insist that there is a fourth possibility, consisting of the possibility that we never achieve AGI and/or we fail to achieve sufficiently physically capable humanoid robots. I am going to reject that possibility. Perhaps I am overly optimistic, but it seems to me that we will eventually attain AGI, and we will eventually attain physically capable humanoid robots.

I shall next respectively consider each of the three genuinely reasonable possibilities.

Option 1: AGI First, Then Humanoid Robots

What if we manage to attain AGI before we manage to achieve physically fluent humanoid robots?

That's just fine.

We would indubitably put AGI to work as a partner with humans in figuring out how we can push along the budding humanoid robot development process. It seems nearly obvious that with AGI's capable assistance, we would overcome any bottlenecks and soon enough arrive at top-notch physically adept humanoid robots.

At that juncture, we would then toss AGI into the humanoid robots and have ourselves quite an amazing combination.

Option 2: Humanoid Robots First, Then AGI

Suppose that we devise very physically adept humanoid robots but have not yet arrived at AGI.

Are we in a pickle?

Nope.

We could use conventional advanced AI inside those humanoid robots. The combination would certainly be good enough for a wide variety of tasks. The odds are that we would need to be cautious about where such robots are utilized. Nonetheless, we would have essentially walking, talking, and productive humanoid robots.

If AGI never happens, oh well, we end up with pretty good humanoid robots. On the other hand, once we arrive at AGI, those humanoid robots will be stellar. It's just a matter of time.

Option 3: AGI And Humanoid Robots At The Same Time

Let's consider the potential of AGI and humanoid robots perchance being attained around the same time. Assume that this timing isn't due to an outright cross-mixing with each other. They just so happen to advance on a similar timeline.

I tend to believe that's the most likely of the three scenarios.

Here's why.

First, despite all the hubris about AGI being within earshot, perhaps in the next year or two, which is a popular pronouncement by many AI luminaries, I tend to side with recent surveys of AI developers that put the date around the year 2040. Some AI luminaires sneakily play with the definition of AGI in hopes of making their predictions come true sooner, akin to moving the goalposts to easily score points.

Second, if you are willing to entertain the year 2040 as a potential date for achieving AGI, that's about 15 years from now. In my estimation, the advancements being made in humanoid robots will readily progress such that by 2040 they will be very physically adept. Probably be sooner, but let's go with the year 2040 for ease of contemplation.

In my view, we will likely have humanoid robots doing well enough that they will be put into use prior to arriving at AGI. The pinnacle of robust humanoid robots and the attainment of AGI will roughly coincide with each other.

Two peas in a pod.

Impact Of Enormous Consequences

There are enormous consequences of having AGI paired with fully physically capable humanoid robots.

As noted above, this will have a humongous impact on white-collar work and blue-collar work. There will be gargantuan economic impacts, societal impacts, cultural impacts, and so on.

Some final thoughts for now.

A single whammy is already being hotly debated. The debates currently tend to be preoccupied with the loss of white-collar jobs due to the attainment of AGI. A saving grace seems to be that at least blue-collar jobs are going to be around and thriving, even once AGI is attained. The world doesn't seem overly gloomy if you can cling to the upbeat posture that blue-collar tasks remain intact.

The double whammy is a lot more to take in.

But the double whammy is the truth. The truth needs to be faced. If you are having doubts as a human about the future, just remember the famous words of Vince Lombardi: "Winners never quit, and quitters never win."

Humankind can handle the double whammy.

APPENDIX

APPENDIX A
TEACHING WITH THIS MATERIAL

The material in this book can be readily used either as a supplemental to other content for a class or it can also be used as a core set of textbook material for a specialized class. Classes, where this material is most likely used, include any classes at the college or university level that want to augment the class by offering thought-provoking and educational essays about AI.

In particular, here are some aspects for class use:

- Computer Science. Studying applications of AI/ML, GenAI, etc.
- Business. Exploring AI in the mental health industry, etc.
- Law. Identifying how AGI will be shaped due to existing and future laws and regulations.

Specialized classes at the undergraduate and graduate level can also make use of this material.

For each chapter, consider whether you think the chapter provides material relevant to your course topic. There is plenty of opportunity to get the students thinking about the topic and force them to decide whether they agree or disagree with the points offered and positions taken. I would also encourage you to have the students do additional research beyond the chapter material presented (I provide next some suggested assignments they can do).

RESEARCH ASSIGNMENTS ON THESE TOPICS

Your students can find background material on these topics, doing so in various business and technical publications. I list below the top-ranked AI-related journals. For business publications, I would suggest sources such as the Harvard Business Review, Forbes, Fortune, WSJ, and the like.

Here are some suggestions for homework or projects that you could assign to students:

a) Assignment for foundational AI research topic: Research and prepare a paper and a presentation on a specific aspect of AGI that involves Generative AI, Machine Learning, Large Language Models, etc. The paper should cite at least 3 reputable sources. Compare and contrast to what has been stated in this book.

b) Assignment for Law classes: Research and prepare a paper on the legal sphere and how it will impact AGI. Cite at least 3 reputable sources and analyze the characterizations. Compare and contrast to what has been stated in this book.

c) Assignment for a Business topic: Research and prepare a paper and a presentation on the business side of AGI, especially as impacted by the latest in AI. What is hot, and what is not? Cite at least 3 reputable sources. Compare and contrast to the depictions in this book.

d) Assignment to do a Startup: Have the students prepare a paper about how they might startup a business in this realm. They must submit a suitable Business Plan for the startup. They could also be asked to present their Business Plan and must have a presentation deck to coincide with it.

You can certainly adjust the aforementioned assignments to fit your particular needs and the class structure. You'll notice that I ask for 3 reputable cited sources for the paper writing-based assignments. I usually steer students toward "reputable" publications, since otherwise they will cite some oddball source that has no credentials other than that they happened to write something and post it onto the Internet. You can define "reputable" in whatever way you prefer, for example, some faculty think Wikipedia is not reputable while others believe it is reputable and allow students to cite it.

The reason that I usually ask for at least 3 citations is that if the student only does one or two citations they usually settle on whatever they happened to find the fastest. By requiring three citations, it usually seems to force them to look around, explore, and end up probably finding five or more, and then whittling it down to 3 that they will actually use.

I have not specified the length of their papers, and leave that to you to tell the students what you prefer. For each of those assignments, you could end-up with a short one to two pager, or you could do a dissertation length paper. Base the length on whatever best fits for your class, and the credit amount of the assignment within the context of the other grading metrics you'll be using for the class.

I mention in the assignments that they are to do a paper and prepare a presentation. I usually try to get students to present their work. This is a good practice for what they will do in the business world. Most of the time, they will be required to prepare an analysis and present it. If you don't have the class time or inclination to have the students present, then you can of course cut out the aspect of them putting together a presentation.

If you want to point students toward highly ranked journals in AI, here's a list of the top journals as reported by various citation counts sources (this list changes from year to year):

- Communications of the ACM
- Artificial Intelligence
- Cognitive Science
- IEEE Transactions on Pattern Analysis and Machine Intelligence
- Foundations and Trends in Machine Learning
- Journal of Memory and Language
- Cognitive Psychology
- Neural Networks
- IEEE Transactions on Neural Networks and Learning Systems
- IEEE Intelligent Systems
- Knowledge-based Systems
- Annual Review of Clinical Psychology
- Health Psychology Review
- JAMA Psychiatry
- Evidence-Based Mental Health
- Etc.

GUIDE TO USING THE CHAPTERS

For each of the chapters, I provide next some various ways to use the chapter material. You can assign the tasks as individual homework assignments, or the tasks can be used with team projects for the class. You can easily layout a series of assignments, such as indicating that the students are to do item "a" below for say Chapter 1, then "b" for the next chapter of the book, and so on.

a) What is the main point of the chapter and describe in your own words the significance of the topic,

b) Identify at least two aspects in the chapter that you agree with, and support your concurrence by providing at least one other outside researched item as support; make sure to explain your basis for disagreeing with the aspects,

c) Identify at least two aspects in the chapter that you disagree with, and support your disagreement by providing at least one other outside researched item as support; make sure to explain your basis for disagreeing with the aspects,

d) Find an aspect that was not covered in the chapter, doing so by conducting outside research, and then explain how that aspect ties into the chapter and what significance it brings to the topic,

e) Interview a specialist in industry about the topic of the chapter, collect from them their thoughts and opinions, and readdress the chapter by citing your source and how they compared and contrasted to the material,

f) Interview a relevant academic professor or researcher in a college or university about the topic of the chapter, collect from them their thoughts and opinions, and readdress the chapter by citing your source and how they compared and contrasted to the material,

g) Try to update a chapter by finding out the latest on the topic, and ascertain whether the issue or topic has now been solved or whether it is still being addressed, explain what you come up with.

ABOUT THE AUTHOR

Dr. Lance B. Eliot, Ph.D., MBA is a globally recognized AI scientist and thought leader, an experienced executive and leader, a successful entrepreneur, and a noted scholar on AI/ML, including his *Forbes* and *AI Trends* columns have amassed over 8.7+ million views, his books on AI are frequently ranked in the Top 10 of all-time AI books, his articles are widely cited, and has developed and implemented dozens of advanced AI systems.

He currently serves as the CEO of Techbruim, Inc. and has over twenty years of industry experience including serving as a corporate officer in billion-dollar-sized firms and as a partner in a major consulting firm. He is also a successful entrepreneur having founded, ran, and sold several high-tech startups.

Dr. Eliot previously hosted the popular radio show *Technotrends* which was also available on American Airlines flights via their in-flight audio program, he has made appearances on CBS 60 Minutes and CNN, has been a frequent speaker at industry conferences, and his podcasts have been downloaded over 300,000 times.

A former professor at the University of Southern California (USC), he founded and led an innovative research lab on Artificial Intelligence. He also previously served on the faculty of the University of California Los Angeles (UCLA) and was a visiting professor at other major universities including serving as Fellow in AI at Stanford University. He was elected to the International Board of the Society for Information Management (SIM), a prestigious association of over 3,000 high-tech executives worldwide.

He has performed extensive community service, including serving as Senior Science Adviser to the Congressional Vice-Chair of the Congressional Committee on Science & Technology. He has served on the Board of the OC Science & Engineering Fair (OCSEF), where he is also has been a Grand Sweepstakes judge, and likewise served as a judge for the Intel International SEF (ISEF). He served as the Vice-Chair of the Association for Computing Machinery (ACM) Chapter, a prestigious association of computer scientists. Dr. Eliot has been a shark tank judge at start-up pitch competitions and served as a mentor for several incubators and accelerators in Silicon Valley and Silicon Beach.

Dr. Eliot holds a Ph.D., MBA, and Bachelor's in Computer Science, and earned the CDP, CCP, CSP, CDE, and CISA certifications.

ADDENDUM

Promises And Perils Of Artificial General Intelligence

Practical Advances in Artificial Intelligence and Machine Learning

By

Dr. Lance B. Eliot, MBA, PhD

For special orders of this book, contact:

LBE Press Publishing

Email: LBE.Press.Publishing@gmail.com

Made in United States
Orlando, FL
04 November 2026

90204697R00114